M000199124

THE MIDNiGHT SHOW

bohemians, byways & bonfires

GladEye Press

© 2022 Nancy Cole

The Midnight Show: bohemians, byways & bonfires

All rights reserved. No part of this book may be reproduced in any form, by photocopying or by any electronic or mechanical means, including information storage or retrieval systems, without permission in writing from both the copyright owner and the publisher of this book.

Published by: GladEye Press
Text Design and Layout: J.V. Bolkan
Cover Design: Sharleen Nelson
Copyediting: GladEye Press
ISBN-13: 978-1-951289-04-1
Library of Congress Control Number: 2022944495

Printed in the United States of America.
10 9 8 7 6 5 4 3

Photos are from Ms. Cole's personal collection, except where noted. Cover photo by Roger Beck, back cover author photo by Rachel Hadiashar.
The body text is presented in Garamond 11 point.

Praise for The Midnight Show

"From the opening scene, this extraordinary life story reads like Jeanette Walls imagined by Neil Gaiman. Cole takes us by the hand, tells her story with rare warmth and humor, and leaves us with the sense that with the right lens, our own lives must be as peculiar and wonderful. Enthusiastically recommended."

— Bob Bickford, author of *A Blueberry Moon for Corah*

"Wow, I stayed up late reading it . . . it's gripping, and really tells a story that most people will never experience—the bus world and the tangled relationship agony . . . wow. I think it reads really great . . . an incredible job illuminating the hippie ethics and unrealities that we all took as doctrine for how life should be. Big Cheers! Well done. Wow."

— Carolyn "Mountain Girl" Garcia

"Cole makes the alchemic, quantum leap from past to present, evoking the sentiment of what a short, strange trip it's been. Tightly written, Cole's book adroitly addresses the joy and freedom of the good times from days gone by, and does a hypnotically fine job of making those days once again come alive—not just on the page—but in the minds of all of those who were there, and all of those who wished they were."

— Cameron Stauth, best-selling author of *In the Name of God*

"What bravery it takes to span a sea change in culture, a great leap between generations—Cole's memoir is an adventure, a reckoning, and an awakening."

— Susan DeFreitas, award-winning author of *Hot Season*

Dedication

My story is dedicated to my grandparents and great aunts
who shared tales about a world long gone; to my mother who
gathered her children around and painted the world of her
childhood on the frozen border between the US and Canada.
All her accounts evoked for us the range of emotions of living
in fear of her father's razor strap, her six older brothers, and of
escaping with her mother and brother during the Depression.

It is also dedicated to the tribe who took me in when I fled
the east coast for the west in the early 1970s—the Bus Farm.
Some of us are still here, some have passed on to the great
caravan of the unknown.

Good friends are the framework to any life. To those who
are gone but left a lasting impression: Judy Varnon, Ginseng
Jack, Roger Beck, Tofu Toby (Alves), Housetruck Al (Anshen),
Nancy Cosper, Greg Fowler, Raisin, and Dave Durant.

And finally, my story would be somewhat boring without
Nicki, MG, Hagen, Stan, my daughter Iris, my late husband
Jim, Lightning, John Anthony, my Hulogosi Publishing
partners, the Oregon Country Fair tribe, and all the friends I've
made in all the roadside attractions along the way.

A special thanks to Shandra Goodpasture Officer for taking
and generously sharing the photographs.

Prologue

On the July day I push my husband's car over the cliff where the street takes that unforgiving turn, I have made a tragic mistake. I fall to my knees in the middle of the street and watch Jim's rattletrap Toyota station wagon fly over the cliff at the bottom of the hill—the place where ordinarily one would slow down and make the turn carefully if they were behind the wheel. Instead, the car, alone in its journey downhill, hovers in midair like a Wile E. Coyote cartoon; the rusted brownish wagon my daughter has dubbed the "Jim-Mobile" plummets out of sight.

There is an earsplitting crash, then a cloud of dust fills the once cloudless sky—the deafening noise of the Jim-Mobile crashing into a blackberry patch far below fills the air like the disaster it is. My hands are now flat to the ground.

I hear a car pull up behind me, turn into our driveway. I am busy praying to the God of Regret, praying for time to back up about 30 seconds so I can reconsider what I've done—pushed the car that wouldn't start so I could hop in and pop the clutch.

Haven't I this done before? I hang my head. I turn to see Ken Kesey at the wheel of an early-model oversized convertible; I hear Mike Hagen's distinctive giggle and wrench myself from the asphalt. Tim Leary, Ken Babbs, Kesey, and Hagen are all leaning over the back of a boat of a car with the top down. They want to know why I'm kneeling in the middle of the road, and what is that enormous dust cloud billowing above the trees down there?

"I was trying to get Jim's car started. He borrowed mine." I have a captive audience.

Hagen gets out. "Where's the car, Camilly?"

They are all waiting for the punchline. But the sound of Hagen's kind voice brings me to tears. His concern is genuine. He's just that kind of guy.

"It wouldn't start," I say, tucking in my shirt, pacing back and forth on center stage in the middle of the street. "I push the car 'till it's pointed downhill ..."

They're all out of the polished green convertible. Ken is a large man with curling and graying hair—a permanent twinkle, a beer gut, a larger-than-life guy. Leary is handsome in an aging gentleman way, eyes pierced and focused on me. Babbs guffaws, piles of brown hair cover his forehead. He's right behind Kesey. Wavy Gravy comes out my front door, wild gray hair, missing front teeth. A roly-poly guy they say was once as good looking as any leading man. He's staying with us for a few days while his roadie figures out what's wrong with their Dodge Caravan. They're on the road to promote his bid for president as Nobody—Nobody for President. These guys are here to pick him up—off for an adventure, but they've found some fun right here in the hills.

"... I start 'er rolling. I'm gunna jump in and pop the clutch." I hiccup, swipe at snot and tears.

We all look down the hill at the dust cloud still hovering in front of the backdrop of a sky once so clear and blue it could have cracked open. "I run to get in, but it takes off; I run faster—it rolls faster and the last I saw ... " Again, all heads turn toward the dust starting to settle over the blackberry patch.

"Nooooo . . . " They say in unison.

I put my head on Hagen's shoulder who has come to comfort me. I know he feels my pain, but these other gray-haired jokers, Pranksters you might say, have found themselves some fun and a good gut laugh.

A man holding a tennis racket runs up the street toward us. I think there's a tennis court down there and this man is yelling in a language I don't understand, maybe Japanese. I don't know, but he's pretty upset. The car just missed the house at the ninety-degree curve, and it's probably his house, and he probably felt the gust of wind as the car flew past his tennis court. I'm sure Jim's car is buried for good in the brambles, but I'm still not sure if I've killed anyone.

The harder these Merry Pranksters laugh, the louder the man in the tennis shorts yells and the more brutal my tears. Someone goes into the house to call Triple A. Someone pulls me out of the street and away from the tennis player and his racket.

We sit around my kitchen table waiting for the tow company. Hagen has retrieved a bottle of vodka from the car and is fixing "drinkie poos." Leary is telling me about his Theory of Chaos—the chaos of our lives and the universe in which we live and how we try to engineer the chaos. We discuss reality and perception. I wonder how this pandemonium he has stumbled upon in the middle of the road on the top of a hill fits his philosophy.

I want to say I'm not someone whose nature it is to depend on anyone else to solve my problems. The inexplicable and mysterious disorder of my life is of my own making for sure, and apparently hilarious to these guys, but Leary seems to get it. I feel his compassion. I say nothing; I'm glad the girls are not home from school yet as I glower at my skinned knees. Leary says, "You gotta do it all by yourself . . . but you also gotta have a little help sometimes." His smile is warm and affable. His silver hair gleams in a shaft of sunlight coming through the skylight above the table.

Hagen and I were once lovers—the kind who remain lifelong friends. He's part of a gang known as the Merry Pranksters—so is Ken and so is Babbs. Over the years, I've sort of melted into the group through other mutual friends, the way these things happen in small towns, and in those days, Eugene was a small town. Hagen and I would go out to the Kesey farm in Pleasant Hill—to parties where Ken would entertain delighted children with his giant ball of string, to nighttime revelries where we'd drape ourselves in fur and howl at the moon like wolves, to quiet dinners where I met interesting people such as clandestine acid chemist Stanley Owsley.

Sometimes it's difficult to pinpoint how friendships begin. Wavy was at the house visiting our roommate during a stop on his presidential campaign tour. I could go on about these more famous people, but this is my story after all.

Someone yells from outside, "Tow truck is here!" A burly guy is standing next to the plus-size truck at the edge of the cliff. He is shaking his head. It doesn't take him long, once he's crawled through the brambles and bushes and connected the hardware, to hoist the Jim-Mobile out of the depths of the blackberry patch and onto the side of the road. There's no harm to the car except for the four flat tires.

My ego is also bruised. On that day, I had tapped into the chaos of my own life—scratched at the wounds and fears—the sum of growing up Nancy. What was it I was so afraid of there on my knees on the pavement at the top of that hill? A beating? The loss of love? That I may have killed someone?

Old wounds stick around.

1

It's the early 1950s. Picture a sweet braided-hair six-year-old girl who runs barefoot in the dirt, tears through the neighborhood of her ancestors on her two-wheel bike. She tells lies, wets the bed, and struggles to survive in an adult world.

She knows her father loves her. Barely out of his own childhood, he wears a Navy aviator jacket, aviator sunglasses—remnants of the recent war—and a DA haircut. He is her hero. He teaches her how to ride the red and blue two-wheel bike with the balloon tires when she's three years old. He takes off the training wheels one day and runs alongside. She sails down Parsons Drive before she realizes he's no longer holding on. He has set her free, and she flies. From that day on, she rides that bike like a terror up and down and around the streets where her father before her, and her grandmother before him, played as children. Parsons Drive is named for her great grandfather, Willis Parsons. In her grandmother's day, it was nothing but dirt farm roads and orchards—the family farm, acres of prime farmland on the western edge of Syracuse. In her father's day, houses had started to appear—Willis had sold lots for houses with a vision of starting a community. He donated a nine-acre cherry orchard on what was now called Cherry Road for the purpose of a community school.

His dreams would come to fruition through the toil of his daughter, my great aunt Marion, my hero, my grandmother of sorts. Dad would attend that school, as would I. My Aunt Helen and Uncle David (twins) were two of the first students. When my dad was a kid, there were still plenty of empty fields where he cut through to his grandparent's house—the house where I spent my formative years, the place where I explored the attic and uncovered magical children's books from the nineteenth century. I felt the spirits of my ancestors in that dusty attic. By the time I was alive, this was a neighborhood on the west side of Syracuse, like any of its time—buses running up and down the streets that were no longer farm roads.

One day, Dad carries me on his shoulders over to McArdle's gas station, one or two blocks up from our house on the corner of West Genesee Street and Parsons Drive. He sits me on the Nehi cooler, places a bottle of ice-cold grape soda in my hands, and heads upstairs to hang with his high school buddies. They are all back from the war. They laugh loudly, and I listen, carefully searching for clues, wondering what they're laughing about.

He has told me to stay right there, to be quiet. This is outlaw territory. I keep quiet all right and would have stopped breathing if I could. Cars whiz by while I clutch the wet soda pop in the glass bottle and examine the contents of the garage. I listen. I look from corner to corner at all the greasy rags and jacks, wooden boxes filled with wrenches and other strange tools. I look down into the dark pit where the empty lift lay in wait for the next car. Like me, it's waiting. I wonder why he's gone up those stairs—what's up there. It's not for me to know, and I accept that with all my heart.

It smells like tires and greasy rags. Fan belts and tire irons hang on the wall on the other side of the pit. Dad told me what they were once. He's gone for a long time, and he and Eddie and Bob and the rest of them are making more noise, laughing louder. My stomach is warm at the thought of Dad having a good time despite the cold bottle in my hands.

On the way home, I ask what he was doing up there for so long. "Oh, just visiting Hank."

"Who's Hank?"

"A friend."

I accept this nonanswer, and he slides me off his shoulders and onto our front porch. I forget about this Hank until one day he shows up at the front door. My mother lets him in. Dad isn't there, but Hank doesn't leave. Later on, she says Hank will be sleeping in the playroom and not to bother him. He doesn't speak English and has funny eyes. He stays in the playroom with the door shut, day after day, but when I knock,

McArdle's gas station, probably early 1950s.

he opens it just enough to slide me a piece of Double Bubble gum, beaming and giggling. After a while, we do this every day—I take the gum to the bottom of the stairs, unwrap it, and wonder about Hank.

It's early one morning when I open my eyes and sense a certain emptiness in our three-story, two-family house. I jump from my bed and run past Hank's room and down the long hallway to my parent's room. The door is wide open, and the bed is empty and neatly made as though no one has slept there. I run down the long staircase and through the house—my footsteps echo from the towering walls of the old house. I pull open the kitchen door and hammer on Aunt Helen's door across the back hall. She and Uncle Ed live on the other side of the big house. In those days they called them two-family houses. My knocks ring empty in the way that knocking does when no one is home. I tear back through our side of the house, up the stairs, back down the hall and pound on Hank's door. I hear him in there. His door opens a crack; he's grinning and hands me the gum.

"Where's my dad?" Hank titters and snorts and then closes the door.

I shuffle back down the hallway, trying to understand what's going on. I slide down the long wooden stairway, clumping my footed pajamas one step at a time until I reach the bottom step and pluck myself down; I unwrap the waxy paper, slowly so it will be perfectly whole. I examine each cartoon frame over and over, waiting for a sound, waiting for something.

Hours may have passed, but I don't move from the stairs. This is where Dad sometimes retrieves me late at night and puts me back to bed or lets me come into the living room and sit on his lap. It's starting to get dark when Aunt Helen sails into the room and scoops me into her arms. It's a baby girl!

I leave with Helen through the upstairs door into her side of the house, past the door to Hank's room that will now be the nursery. I never saw Hank again.

After Mary is born, I spend more and more time on my own while Dad is at work, my mother in her room with the door shut, Mary on her back in the middle of a wooden playpen in the big old living room.

I try to fix breakfast, but always set something on fire or make myself bleed. My mother flies downstairs in great rages and fits. In those days, toasters were not yet designed to automatically pop toast up into the air when it was done.

Me, age 4.

If you knew what you were doing, you would set the bread in an upright position against a heating coil until it was perfectly toasted, turn the slice over and do the same on the other side. If you were four or five years old, you might fill a three-story house with smoke, enough smoke to raise the dead. After my mother threatens me with mayhem a few times, I give up on toast, on sliced oranges, on taking breakfast altogether. I feel my parent's love slipping away. I am alone.

I begin wandering the neighborhood early in the morning. One neighbor woman serves me toast covered with a thick layer of butter and globs of jelly. I eat it despite a gag reflex at the sight of it. Another, the mother of a cheerful gang of children, tells me stories about how they save baby birds fallen from the cedar tree out front, about building a fort in the cherry tree out back. Mrs. Merriweather, always in high spirits, reminds me of the mother in my Little Golden Book, *The Happy Family*.

More and more Dad is angry with me. Like the morning when I must have been around six and burned toast again because my sister was hungry. Smoke filled the house all the way to the attic this time. He opens the back door, swishing it back and forth, scowling. My sister, Mary, is squeezed into her highchair over in the corner; she laughs and Dad snorts.

After he leaves for work, Mom comes downstairs in her blue terry cloth bathrobe. She sits at the kitchen table sipping coffee in silence. I nibble chunks of cold cereal, watch her lift the percolator, bubbles bursting inside the glass dome at the top of the pot; watch her pour steaming coffee into the flowered China cup with the matching saucer.

"Get dressed, Nancy." She raises her eyebrows. "Sally Bennett invited me for coffee. You can play with Carol Ann." She stares at the mess on the counter; yanks on her bathrobe sash, glowers at the surface of her coffee; she sips again, and then blows on the hot dark liquid. Her gaze wanders out the window, fixes on a spot somewhere in the backyard. She holds the coffee cup in front of her mouth, blowing, staring, sipping, leaning on her elbows, blowing, sipping, and blowing again. Some mornings she smokes cigarettes. Today, she just sips and stares.

Mary starts to fuss. I carry her cereal bowl to the sink; unlatch her, wondering, as I wrestle her from the choke hold of the highchair, if Mom will yell at me for not cleaning the crumbs. But she is still staring out the window when we leave the kitchen. I can picture us, hand in hand, those pink and blue seersucker summer pajamas.

The Bennets' dark brown shuttered house towers above the corner, one block away on the corner of Cherry Road and Genesee Street. My grandmother once told me that when she was little, this street was a two lane dirt road connecting one end of New York State to the other and was traveled by horse-drawn buggies and wagons. Then it was called the Genesee Turnpike. Now it's a busy street, a dangerous street, according to the adults. "Stay away from that road, Nancy; don't even walk in the ditch." Usually, I cut through old lady Losey's backyard. No sidewalk for the stroller, Mom carries Mary, and I pull the heavy contraption across the Losey's front lawn.

A tray of coffee and biscuits are arranged on a wicker table beneath a gigantic maple tree in the Bennets' backyard. Smoke from Sally's cigarette curls up and around an umbrella of leaves, swirling through shafts of sunlight and disappearing into the trees.

"Nancy, keep an eye on Mary. Do you hear me?" They want to smoke and laugh, and is was my job to keep my sister out of their hair.

Carol Ann and I sit in the soft cool grass, pushing a croquet ball back and forth while our moms carry on like one train engine trying to catch up with another—bursts of laughter, like sudden blasts at railroad crossings, hurt my ears. Mary sits a ways off watching us.

Carol Ann walks away, and I watch a grasshopper climbing through the grass. She calls from behind the hedge, and I run the length of it and find her sitting cross-legged on a blanket feeding her Tiny Tears doll. She has a miniature glass baby bottle filled with water; I long to have one. "You can sit on the blanket too," she says. Her bossiness makes her eyes look like the cat peering from behind the bushes.

"This blanket stinks," I say.

Carol Ann turns the doll upside down. "It's supposed to pee when you feed it. Stupid doll." I follow her back to the mothers to find out why the doll will not pee.

"Where's Mary?" Mom is crushing a cigarette into an ashtray overflowing with butts. "I asked you a question, Nancy, where is your sister?"

Before I can say anything, the two women leap from the faded chairs and we're all running and shouting, racing toward the splashing sounds coming from the fishpond. Mary looks like an enormous, injured bird floating on her stomach in the slimy green water in the mossy cement pond. Her flowered cotton dress spreads like wings on a dead bird fallen from a tree. I've never seen my mother move like that. She jumps into the pond, shoes and all, crushing lily pads, plunging toward my sister floating so still in the center of the pool. She heaves her out of the darkness, out of the murky water pouring off her and out of her.

By the time my father is home from work that night, Mary is sleeping in her crib. I hear him from my bedroom when he comes in the back door. Mom's muffled voice echoes through the house—wafts up the stairs like smoke from burnt toast. She's telling him how I almost let my sister drown.

The house is quiet. A fly buzzes on the sill next to my open window. Cars pass on the street out front in a steady rhythm and flow. I edge across the floor, trying to avoid the creaky spots; put my ear on the heat grate. Nothing. I climb back onto the bed; open *Alice in Wonderland* and read what the cat said several times, but nothing sinks in. My head spins. I turn pages and listen to Dad's footsteps on the stairs. Will he give me "The Look" or will he spank me? The door opens, and we stare at each other in silence for what feels like a long time.

"Guess you had a rough day?" He pushes the door open all the way but doesn't move.

"Yes." I look down at the book—don't want to be looking at him when he yells, when he tells me how bad I am, how I let him down again. I've heard it all.

"Nancy?"

Dad and me, circa 1954.

Cherry Road School, circa 1925.

"Yes?" I can see the pack of Lucky Strikes in the pocket of his white summer shirt as he strides across the room.

I flinch, but he just sits on the bed and puts his arm around me. I keep staring at the book—the pages a blur of color. My ears are ringing. I can't hear what he's saying. Tears drip onto the rabbit who's lifting his watch fob into the air.

"Look at me, Nancy."

His eyes were soft and blue that afternoon; they held mine and he stroked my back. I can still feel the stabbing pain in my throat. I can still feel the urge to wrap my arms around his neck and tell him I love him. He says something like, "Life is confusing sometimes. All I ask is that you do your best." Then he left. Then it was over, and the door clicked shut.

My childhood was an endless attempt to win my father's love—an affection fading like an unexpected sunset in the middle of the afternoon. Then, the worst of the worst happened. We moved. We moved to a strange town, away from all that I had ever known, away from the ancestral place where my grandmother grew up during the last century, where I played in the remnants of my great grandfather's orchard.

Great Aunt Marion built the red brick schoolhouse in the cherry orchard in the 1920s. The first year the kids had class in a nearby hen house. The next year came a two-story school in what had been her father's cherry orchard. My father and aunts and uncles had gone to Cherry Road School, and now I did too. I rode my bike each morning the few blocks between our house and the school.

I loved Marion—my great aunt who was more of a grandmother—who held me on her lap in the car and let me steer the rumbling ship as we sang choruses of "Lonely Little Petunia"

Me and Aunt Marion Parsons.

on our way to Marble Farms Dairy where we ate black walnut or black raspberry ice cream cones. Spending the night at her house was the chocolate sundae of my life. I felt loved and cared for. I was safely in the hands of someone who washed my face with a warm washcloth before tucking me into my own little bed—told me stories of her childhood. I soaked in the tales of the olden days, about hitching up the horse and buggy, about the hired help in the orchards.

I came home from school one day, leaned my bike against the railing on the back porch, and walked up the familiar steps. The old screen door creaked, and I paused, held the door, held my breath.

"Don't let the flies in Nancy." Like burglars, my mother, Aunt Marion, and three strange men were gathered in the kitchen. The towering men in dark suits took up all the space, all the air.

They didn't notice me following behind Marion as they all walked boldly from room to room. They said older houses had little value anymore because women want to live in new houses now. Marion wore her schoolhouse reserve, signaling me to be quiet. But when I edged in close, she put her hand on my shoulder. I listened to the conversation about the dentist who wanted to buy the house. Because he was young and struggling, because this was such an old house in need of repairs and extensive remodeling required to set up his practice, he couldn't offer near as much as we were asking.

Not long after that day, we must have been taking our Sunday drive, but this time instead of a visit to Grandma's, we were house hunting. I can now picture Mary and me in the back seat of Dad's old Dodge, the one that had been Marion's until it wore out. We were on our knees looking out the back window. I must have been about seven years old and she about three. We were straining to see out the window. The back of the wool seat smelled like wet mittens. Dad wound the car around the curved streets up behind the hillside above what was once the family's dairy farm and apple orchard—the one that had been sold a long time ago after my great grandfather and his cousins died—when there was a Depression and a war; they did what they had to do. Now people were building a neighborhood of ranch-style houses up there with picture windows and wall-to-wall carpeting.

"I would be so happy, Pete, with wall-to-wall and a picture window," my mother crooned. "Can you imagine? A brand-new kitchen with brand-new linoleum; I would keep a kitchen like that so clean." Mom sighed. The side of my father's face tensed; his jaw muscles flexed. He was not so sure—I could tell. But it was out of his hands.

People like my parents wanted to settle in these new kinds of houses and neighborhoods. They wanted to escape something—maybe the great aunts, maybe the braided rugs, maybe they just wanted something different. They had no axe to grind. They had fought for the right to live life on their own terms. I remember hearing the aunts cluck their tongues, but always out of earshot of Dad.

The decade of my childhood was the peak of the post-war economy—20-year mortgages, 3.5 children, the Baby Boom, and a new kind of manufacturing industry that was putting money in people's pockets, feeding the economy, feeding people's urges to keep up with the Joneses. In the battlefields of WWII, young men had dreamed of having this life. They wrote to their gals back home who had said they would wait. When it all came to pass, when the war was over, the young couples were not satisfied with the old ways. They wanted something better, they wanted to be on their own, and soon they were earning enough money to make it so.

The search for the new house grew wider and farther away from the place I knew as home. "I don't want to go! Why do we have to go?! Can't we stay here? Can I stay with Marion?" I cried all the way.

I hated the small village near the basin of the Finger Lakes. Today they call it quaint—churches on every corner of downtown, one streetlight, everything a little rundown. It was all strange. On my first day at the new school, the teacher pinched my chin and shook my head when I left my sneakers on the desk. But my parents were happy on the dead-end street filled with families like ours. My father joined the volunteer fire department. They played checkers and drank beer in the firehouse in the center of town across from the Methodist church. Once in a while, they put out a grass fire. In the fall, they organized annual homecoming bonfires. I remember the terror of being pulled by a stranger's hand in front of me and pushed by the stranger behind me as we looped up one street and down another during the annual snake dance. I stood shaking behind the crowd when we finally reached the raging fire in the middle of the football field up on the hill.

There were Halloween parades down Main Street, sugar-covered donuts, and apple cider at the firehouse. My costume was always covering my eyes—blinded in an already dark world; I had lost my roots, but the tragedy was mine alone.

Eventually I settled in, and memories of this place are filled with sounds of mothers calling their children, lush maple trees, trucks roaring toward the lumber yard and parades of school buses headed toward the school; filled with memories of the aromas of wildflowers, grasses, and berries in the fields; the pungent odor of pine in the little woods across the street; sounds of the creek lapping over rocks and boulders; the little mill train that ran down below our street two times a day. I liked to climb down there and wait for it to go by, popping tar bubbles in the street as I went and shimmying down the cliff just in time to wave at the engineer of the tiny train who always waved back.

My father's anger filled the air in our house until there was nothing left to breathe. My parents yelled back and forth over us kids' heads. Their fights came like explosions, erupting from my mother in a litany of what we had done, how hard she worked, how awful we were. By the time I was eight, there were two more babies. Sometimes his anger and frustration broke out at the dinner table, mashed potatoes and Dad's fists flying; mushy cooked frozen peas flew to the floor—a theater of chaos.

I'd hide out in my room and daydream that Aunt Marion was my mother—a kindly mother who complimented my small achievements, took me to lunch at Shraft's, and bought me pretty dresses downtown—the best dresses in the best stores. She would tuck me in at night with a kiss. But I was certain, in fact, that I was not lovable, not worthy, not really. I kept to myself.

Sometimes my father was kind, and those times stay with me more than the bad ones. One afternoon, I was walking across the front yard after school, and he was pulling something out of the backseat of the car with a big grin on his face. Then he headed toward me pushing a brand-new shiny blue bike. One time in the dark of a cold winter night, he stood on the back porch in his shirt sleeves and watched me ski down the back hill, cheering me on, over and over. Once, he drove me down to Syracuse in the dark to audition for the play, *Gypsy Rose Lee*. I felt his love and pride as he stood in the hall and listened to me belt out "Let Me Entertain You." Clearly,

I was far too young to play this part, 13 or 14, but it was the doing of it that counted, and he knew that.

2

My mother was the ninth of ten children who survived a frozen landscape and hunger—in fear of their father's razor strap in the coldest spot in the country, International Falls, Minnesota. Of six brothers and four sisters, eight made it to adulthood. One brother died in the war. By the time Mom was born, her mother, Ella Coffin MacPherson, was sick and tired. Mom's father, Jack MacPherson, was a notorious drunk, embarrassing the family, falling into the frigid northern waters during annual log rolling contests, carousing in the dark corners of taverns and pool halls. In the winter, the temperature rarely reached 10 degrees Celsius. Jack failed to keep steady work, terrorized his children, drunk or sober, and ran his small army of MacPherson children by the switch.

One hot summer afternoon during the first decade of the 20th century, Ella came around the side of the small clapboard house carrying a basket of laundry. She screamed, dropped the basket. Her oldest daughter, Viannah, was hurdling thirty feet into the air above the street. She hit the pavement, cracking her head like an egg. The little MacPherson girl with the long dark braids had run into the street for a chunk of ice from the ice man's truck. Her younger sister Gladys was watching from the front stoop.

As if playing out a tragic concerto, at that exact same moment, Jack MacPherson came weaving up the street. He too saw Viannah fly into the air; saw her crash to the street. He ran with no regard for his weak heart or anything or anyone, gathering the broken and bloody child into his arms, racing, her limp body bouncing to the rhythm of his desperation all the way to the hospital, but it was too late.

The man in the speeding Model-T never stopped.

My mother's and my father's childhoods could not have been more different. Dad's family would have been called affluent, an old and highly-regarded family—landowners, fruit farmers—distinguished. After Mom's father died of a stroke one Christmas Eve during the heat of the depression, Ella kept her brood fed any way she could—once by digging potato peels from the garbage can behind the church rectory. Dad's version of the Depression, on the other hand, was a story about how they had to have their shoes resoled instead of buying new ones for school.

Mom turned fourteen while they still lived—those who had survived— amid the frozen lakes on the border of Canada. Soon after, she and her mother and younger brother left. They rode the train to Richland, Washington. Ella, who was by this time legally blind, had hopes fueled by letters from her brother and sister-in-law, from cousins who had gone on ahead to find jobs at Hanford. This is where they split the atom; this is where they were making the kind of bomb that would settle what was going on in Europe. Mom cried all the way.

They had little money to survive. They moved in with Aunt Josie. Mom was enrolled in a one-room schoolhouse in a small farm town. The roads were nothing but dirt, and the boys wore boots to school. Eventually, she forgot about finishing high school and took a job at the military base to help keep the three of them alive, to help get them out of that house where Aunt Josie, rigid and cold, ran the place like the tyrant she was. Mom wondered if there

Mom and Dad.

was something wrong with her.

She saw an ad in the paper about a job at the army depot. When she went to apply for the job, they asked her if she had ever driven a jeep. She had never driven anything, but out of desperation she lied, and then taught herself after a few jerky attempts. These were desperate times for everyone. Men were going to war. It turned out my mother loved that job at the army depot where she worked for a colonel for two years. I'm guessing this was one of the happiest times of her life; the stories she told us kids were full of humor and pride.

On Saturday nights, Mom and her cousin, Mary Coffin, got dolled up and went to dances at the USO in Pasco where soldiers passed through from all over the country heading to points all over the world. One night, my father, a young boy of seventeen or eighteen from back east, asked her to dance. She had been leaning against the wall, off to the side, tapping her feet, shy and eager. Dad had to work up his nerve, but the two got together that night. Later, as the war played out overseas and he was learning to ride gunner on a Navy bomber plane on the other side of the Pacific Ocean, he couldn't get the young bombshell out from under his skin. He wrote her letters, and she wrote back.

Ella had met a man who didn't want to have children around the house. He had money, a nice house, furniture. She had a future to consider; she sent Mom to live with an older brother in Los Angeles where she found work as a telephone operator at the phone company. Her brother Ray would pick her up after work on the back of his LAPD motorcycle to keep her safe from the streets. She was more afraid of the ride through LA on that speeding bike than anything on the street. She was afraid of the brother.

Once the war was over and my father back in Syracuse, he was itchy to find this beautiful dark-haired girl. No matter how loudly his parents and his aunts objected, he hit the cross-country highway hitchhiking one day in 1946—made it to LA in four days and wasted no time proposing when he arrived on her brother's doorstep. A proper wedding was arranged by one of his mother's cousins who lived in a swanky neighborhood called Beverly Hills. Ethel and Peter returned to Syracuse on the train, and my mother spent the rest of her life missing the family of her childhood, the raucous older brothers and sisters, the house filled with aunts and uncles and cousins—all lost to her long ago, but still lived in her mind; it was all waiting for her if she could only find her way home.

There is one thing my parents did share in common. My father, too, was born into a family who had endured the loss of a child. His older brother, John, who he would never meet, died at the age of six on Christmas Eve, 1920, of the flu pandemic sweeping the globe, killing millions, killing more than had died in the entire Great War. It had come on so fast that a

Left, John Parsons Cole with my grandfather, Claude Cole, Sept 1914. Above, John with my grandmother, Grace Parsons Cole. Below, John on the lap of his grandfather, Willis Parsons with cousins behind.

small cold developed into a vicious pneumonia before a doctor could make it to the house. The precious child was dead in less than 24 hours, leaving my father's parents in a lasting state of grief.

They say that the pain of the loss of a child is generational. Those who come later have no idea how the adults in their world came to be people who snap, who fear, who at times love you deeply, and at times seem to resent your existence.

Several years ago, my father handed me a raggedy photo album. It once belonged to his mother, my grandmother. An artist, she had covered the handmade book of black felt sheets with now-faded flowery fabric. Enthusiastic to have in my possession anything that had belonged to her, I began turning pages, examining each picture of my young grandparents from a long time ago. I had never seen them without gray hair. In these photos they were holding a young boy I did not recognize. Each picture had been carefully labeled: "John's first pony ride," or, "John's first boat ride." Young versions of Grandma and Grandpa smiled with the happiness of an untarnished world—fawning over a beloved child at picnics by a lake, backyard birthday parties with ponies; the boy wrapping his small arms around his father's neck while extended family brought in the hay on a sunny afternoon. On another page the boy fondles his father's tie—the man who would one day be my stern grandfather. He smiles down at his young son. On the back side of one loose picture, written in my grandmother's distinctive script: John Parsons Cole, 1914–1920. I still can't look at those pictures without crying.

Although Christmas was all but ignored by my grandparents, my grandmother read me *Peter Rabbit* and *Charlotte's Web*; she taught me to play the piano while my grandfather rocked in his chair, smoking his pipe. One day, he and I went down to the barn and crafted a make-believe fishing pole with a bamboo stick, twine, and a safety pin. We went down to the lake where I dangled what I believed to be a real fishing pole—with great hopes of catching a fish—into the clear water of Skaneateles Lake.

All those years later, examining that photo album, I discovered a picture of young John with a make-believe fishing pole made from a bamboo pole, twine, and a safety pin. At that moment, I would have given one of my limbs to hold my grandfather's hand and tell him I loved him.

We endure. We grow up. We move on.

It was 1955, and I was seven years old when we moved away from the family farmhouse. I cried all the way to the small village down in the valley, just over the hill from the Finger Lakes. My mother had more babies. Eventually there were five of us. I changed diapers, fed bottles, washed

Young John with his fishing pole.

the dishes. I wandered off, hid out in my room or in the arms of an old apple tree. I meandered around the streets of the village on the banks of Nine Mile Creek. By the time I was a teenager, I roamed the woods in the dark, slept in the back seat of an abandoned car, studied the home life of my friends—curious about how they lived. I was searching for something I couldn't name, running away from something I may have been too young to understand. I had never considered such things as the meaning of life—my life. I had not considered the concept of free will versus fate.

I graduated from high school during the Summer of Love—during a time when there was talk about going to California. A seed was planted, and I was overcome by some irreversible longing to venture off. Eventually I wandered 3,000 miles away, as far as I could go behind the wheel of a car.

My father was generous in certain ways, but our battles stormed on and on. He let me use his car, paid for the gas. I returned the favor by turning the American flag decal on the wing window upside down every time I drove his Chevrolet. A silent war between the two of us—I would turn the flag upside down, and he would turn it back again, over and over until it barely stuck any more, its corners curled and frayed. The Vietnam War raged on, and his generation had not yet understood the consequences, while my generation went off to fight and die or to protest in ways that frightened our parents.

"You know," he said one day after one of my pronouncements about California, "Oregon is a nice place."

Not long after that, I found an atlas at a friend's house, dragged it off the shelf and studied the map of the United States, surprised to discover Oregon was snuggled between California and Washington—instead of beneath Montana as I had believed—right on the Pacific Ocean. I turned pages and found the Oregon state map, placed my finger on a city called Eugene where cartography symbols indicated a university town not far from the coast, surrounded by mountains and rivers. I had no thoughts about destiny or fate, but it was what you might call a pivotal moment.

I had no idea what to expect in this place three thousand miles from home. There was no internet or Google information in the early 1970s. I didn't worry. This was an adventure. I would go back home like I always did.

The lure of antiwar protests, rock concerts, and psychedelic merrymaking had lost their luster by the late 1960s. The Mamas and Papas' "California Dreamin'" got lots of play, and my friends and I dreamt about sunshine, Flower Power, People's Park, and a back-to-earth movement happening on the West Coast. Kids were going to San Francisco and points north and south along the Pacific Ocean.

I dropped out of college during the great student strike following the invasion of Cambodia and slaughter of four college students at Kent State in 1970. I was lost and flailing, but my dream of an escape turned into a plan. One day in early August 1971, my friend Tom and I loaded up my Chevy II station wagon and headed west, carving our own pioneer trail across the

Wyoming above, and Yellowstone, below on the trip to Oregon in 1971.

Great Plains, stopping at roadside attractions—Wall Drug, Mt. Rushmore, the largest buffalo in the world—soaking in the red-hued landscape I had never imagined. I took pictures of the Badlands and the little prairie dogs inhabiting this endless countryside. We burned across the scorching prairies, dousing our sweat with cotton swabs of rubbing alcohol. I kept the bottle in the glove box. When the Rocky Mountains emerged on the horizon, we drove in silence toward the rising snowcapped peaks.

Two summers earlier I had watched a man walk on the moon. These foothills were my own march across a new planet where the sky grew wider and bluer, and the sun sparkled upon brightly lit cornfields waving in the breeze.

3

The here were 75,000 people living in Eugene, Oregon, in 1971 according to the welcome sign. We drove up and down streets where none of the buildings were taller than two or three stories—long-haired hippies everywhere.

Back home, my father and brother had argued endlessly about haircuts.

The Renaissance Fair. Photo by Shandra Goodpasture Officer

Dad would leave a dollar twenty-five on the counter for my brother's haircut, and my brother would pocket the cash. But these guys wandering the streets of Eugene hadn't seen a barber in years, much less a dollar twenty-five.

The first night, we stayed at the Quality Inn just off the main drag. The sign said eight dollars a night, and that seemed reasonable. The next day we rented a one-bedroom apartment up the street. The world was spinning around us. Within hours of moving in, we met Paula, our next-door neighbor who introduced us to her boyfriend, Bill. They were on their way to his sister and brother-in-law's house where they were having a

Country Fair planning meeting. Photographer unknown

party, where they were getting ready to go to the Renaissance Fair, sell chili, have some fun. Would we like to come along?

Our band of new friends included brothers and sisters who had grown up on a dairy farm in the rural hills down in Douglas County in southern Oregon, their spouses and girlfriends, and Paula, Tom, and me. For them, the novelty of new friends from New York drove our alliance. A lot of people we met seemed to think that if you were from New York, even if you insisted it was just Upstate New York, you were from the big city and knew things about the world they did not—pastrami sandwiches, tall buildings, gangsters. I was more interested in tasting my first taco and finding out what this fair was all about.

I soaked it all in as we rumbled down a rutted and bumpy dirt road through a thickly wooded pasture. We emerged onto a sprawling field filled with vans and buses, groups of people walking, shuffling, draped in bags and backpacks, carrying

Along the road at the Country Fair. Photo by Shandra Goodpasture Officer

babies. A few hippies were directing traffic, telling people where to park, where to camp.

I stepped from the car onto the dusty parking lot and was pulled through the front gate by an undertow of flamboyant people—swept away. I forgot about the chili booth where I was supposed to be heading, about Tom, my new friends, about the world on the other side of the woods, and about my life back home. My new fluffy white poodle-terrier puppy, Missy, was snuggled in my pocket.

We meandered through endless dirt paths lined with booths made of old barnwood and twigs. People sat around campfires talking and singing; some wielding hammers and saws, getting ready to open makeshift storefronts the next morning. There were boxes of leather goods piled in the back of one booth, the scent of homemade candles

Welcome to the Oregon Country Fair. Photo by Shandra Goodpasture Officer

The Fair Marching Band. Photo by Shandra Goodpasture Officer

wafted from another. Two guys marched past carrying a pole lined with muslin dresses and shirts. I stopped and listened to three guys playing guitar around a firepit. They motioned for me to sit and join in, and so I did.

By the time I found the chili booth, Bill and Bonnie were in a heated discussion with a woman who was large and in charge. She wore pinstriped coveralls, her hair in braids. She wanted to take our booth down and put the Odyssey Information Booth—Fair Central—in its place. The two women faced off, their voices a decibel louder with each round. I must have daydreamed in the way I did when my parents fought, but when I came back to earth the problem was solved and no one had to move. These were the only raised voices I heard all weekend. I watched as the woman in charge strode back across the grassy meadow surrounding the Main Stage—kids running back and forth with balloons, women with their shirts off twirling in the sun. Throngs of long-haired people were dressed in colorful garb, or no garb at all; they floated past.

The Main Stage meadow at night. Photographer unknown

At the chili booth, cauldrons of red goop simmered on Coleman stoves behind our handmade countertop lined with red-checkered oil cloth. It looked like we were ready for customers. My big blue tent had been erected out behind the booth in a little wooded area. Bonnie kept stirring with a huge wooden spoon. I said I thought something smelled funny; others nodded in agreement. Her brother took a taste of the two-day-old chili but didn't swallow.

Bill and Joe took the tubs of spoiled chili and disposed of the mess somewhere, maybe down the portable toilets clustered at the edge of the woods. End of the chili, but the weekend was just getting started—the constant backdrop a cacophony of music, laughter, shouts, and the hum of murmuring voices. The air had that aroma of spent leaves and grass, and a deeper aroma of dense and mossy woodland.

Missy-dog and I sat in a patch of grass in front of the now defunct chili booth by the side of the path watching the parade pass by. We gazed at people dressed in patched and decorated

37

jeans, flowing scarves—sinuous costumes covered in sparkles and fandangle. Men were mostly shirtless, some had strings of beads hanging on their chests; some wore patchwork, some were covered in muslin—shuffling in the loose straw, some had dirty-faced children in tow. One man sidled past with long-legged strides, like Mr. Natural. He wore nothing but a big grin. One woman in a long, ruffled skirt held two babies in slings on either side of her breasts; she carried dried flowers in a handwoven basket. I had on my Mickey Mouse T-shirt and my favorite bell-bottom jeans I'd embroidered with flowers and borders of color. I may have been barefoot or maybe wearing my Red Wing hiking boots.

When the sun set, the temperature dropped, and crisp autumn air enveloped us as the sun glowed behind the oak trees lining the Long Tom River. Darkness fell on a few hundred people, and the dust-filled air sparkled with lantern light—flashlights, campfires, the roar of the day now but whispers. Later that night, the chili booth crew lined up in my hulking canvas tent like rows of sardines. We giggled and recounted the day. We lay in the dark listening to rhythms emanating from the drum tower until we all passed into dream worlds, rotten chili forgotten. I liked this new place, Oregon.

Tom and I hadn't been in Oregon long when we moved into a little cabin on the side of a rocky hill overlooking a spectacle of green dotted with sheep and cattle that stretched out for miles. We peed and pooped in a little shed he built over a hole out back. He built a fence around the five-acre place; we got a horse, three goats, and a 1946 Dodge pickup truck with running boards and a windshield that pushed out to let in fresh air. I learned to double-clutch, break a horse, and chase goats out of the garden with a shovel. On the way to town, we oohed and awed at the snow-covered Three Sisters mountains peeking up from a distant horizon. I soaked it in like new love.

I fell for Oregon—wildflowers on the hillsides growing between rocks and downed trees, lichen cascading from oak tree branches, moss-covered tree trunks, water dripping from Douglas Fir trees.

Several times in Oregon I'd already had the best meal I'd ever eaten, seen the most magnificent night skies, played in the ocean, met my best friends, met my soul mates, watched the night sky reflect on water, any water—the ocean, a mountain lake, a pond where creatures jumped from the water, splashing, slicing it open.

The hippies next door to our little cabin were digging a well by hand. Farther up the road a collection of yurts, tents, tepees, and school buses marked the hillsides at another commune, the Church of the Creative. We were the most sought after, me and Tom—we had a telephone. When Steven Gaskin from The Farm in Tennessee made a tour stop in our valley, he and his followers ran up a several hundred-dollar phone bill. They promised to pay us back, but who was counting.

By the time spring set in, Tom had taken to drinking and hanging out with other boozers. I wanted to get away from him, away from the little red cabin with the strange noises in the walls. I had taken to sleeping in the living room, but he hardly noticed, passed out on the bed. I could not have put that desire for deeper meaning into words back then, but I wandered away and never came back. Instead, I moved in with two women living in an abandoned schoolhouse up the road.

When I returned to retrieve my belongings, I found my stereo, my ringer washer, and the rest of my things piled out back in the rain. I took a few items and the dog and never looked back.

The old schoolhouse was heated with a woodstove. I learned to chop wood filled with little slivers that got under the skin on my fingers and festered their way out over time. We had chickens, a six-year-old girl of questionable heritage named Serena, and extra tenants who lived in a powder-blue school bus in the driveway. Tucker and Mary made their own cheese. Big balls of aging goats' milk hung from the ceiling, filling the tiny space with a sour aroma. Tucker, a black man twice Mary's age, was prone to wandering. Mary waited for his return, wringing her hands, and making more cheese until I could no longer go in there. We weren't sure what to do about the situation, and decided to let it play out, decided to have a party, and invite everyone in the valley.

The night of the party was the first time I laid eyes on Stan. He was so tall I could see him across the room, pitched high above the heads of all the others. Word had spread about the party. On the night of the festivities, our sprawling timeworn schoolhouse filled with people from up and down the Camas Swale Valley, from the Church of the Creative, the Goat Farm, the Mud Farm, and the Bus Farm.

I watched from the corner of my eyes as the tall lean guy with long dark hair and handlebar mustache headed toward me. We were drawn to each other like penny nails to a magnet and stood together in silence until the evening waned.

As they were leaving, a woman named Judy who had come with Stan and the rest of the Bus Farm mavens, put her arms around me and whispered in my ear, "Come visit." Then she and the crew of bearded men drifted out the back door. Our neighbors took leave, one-by-one, or two-by-two, carrying guitar cases, empty casserole dishes, and sleeping children. The clatters of revving engines filled the dark September night. Pickups, flatbeds, and Volkswagen vans jostled down our rutted driveway, past the blue school bus and onto the main road.

I stood there in the dark watching my new friends disappear into the night, the tops of their trucks and vans lit by moonlight.

These were lean times, so when the invitation came for dinner at the Bus Farm, I was eager to accept. That night I ate my first bowl of lentil soup, and possibly because I had been on the verge of starvation, it tasted like the best meal I ever ate.

The tall guy sat next to me during the potluck meal in the farmhouse where Bus Farm people shared the kitchen and one bathroom; the living room was a central meeting place. Young families lived in refurbished school buses and Victorian houses constructed atop flatbed trucks and converted step vans that covered the hillside on the outskirts of a tiny Oregon cow town, 50 miles from the coast, 50 miles from the Cascade

Jack and Judy's Bus. Photo by Roger Beck

Mountains, 100 miles from the Columbia River Gorge, and a couple hundred miles from the High Desert.

The night of the potluck, he and I hardly spoke, but when it was time to go home, the lanky guy followed when I headed for the door, said he'd take a look at my '53 Chevy coupe. I told him it was stalling, skipping, and that I had changed the water pump. He said he would look under the hood if I brought it by tomorrow.

I am back at the Bus Farm early the next afternoon, maneuvering my Army-green tank with caution, but a bit of abandon, into a muddy downsloped driveway, the commune now visible in the clear light of the fresh autumn day.

He's out the door before I turn off the car, and I wonder if he's been waiting for me. In no time, we are bantering about my Chevy. He says cut the engine; he says turn it back on. He fiddles under the hood of my rattletrap. I love my car, a three-on-the-column clunker. It reminds me of the car my mother learned to drive in, my father yelling and waving his arms like a street cop as she tried to shift, veering across traffic into a dusty parking lot while we kids huddled in fear for our lives in the backseat.

I remember it: steep and muddy potholed driveway lined with school buses and house trucks in various stages of construction. Stan's bus just a yellow school bus—the seats pulled out; a plywood platform in the back, mattress piled with old blankets, little round woodstove in the middle; no curtains or furniture to make it look like a home. I am mentally designing curtains and pillows.

The original yellow bus sits on the hill at the old Bus Farm.

Across the driveway, a bus painted forest green looks older, road worn. Judy and Ginseng Jack and little Aimee live in this converted 1940s White. Judy invites us in for tea and rice and vegetables. Inside, hanging herbs, scraps of fabric, and wooden dishes line the walls, hang from the ceiling. It smells like cookies and oranges. Dark as a cave, the floor is covered with old, flowered carpeting. Thick green velvet curtains keep out the light and the view from the road; I can't stop staring. Judy, a small woman with long hair and a solid frame, is cooking squash, onions, and something called tofu in a large pot called a wok. Stan suggests maybe she could show me how to make rice, and a flicker of my abandoned life back east crosses the movie screen in my mind. Women's rights? So what. I'm eager to be part of this scene, and if making rice is the membership fee, I'm game.

After lunch, he takes me around; introduces me to a guy named Logan who is up on the roof of a dark-green bus with lots of wood trim he shares with Debbie, a bubbly girl with red cheeks. Logan is trying to latch the skylight before they take off for the coast.

We amble on down the lineup of house trucks. Onie and Toby's chimney juts from the roof of their cedar shake-covered bus, aims like a crooked arrow toward the blue autumn sky; smoke wafts from a kitchen fire that keeps the bus warm for two babies. Big eyed and smiling in a way I've never seen in my own little brothers, Jonah and Olem crawl around on the soft Persian carpet, up and down on benches upholstered in patchwork and velveteen scraps. Toby, barefooted despite the chilly afternoon, her long black hair is wrapped into plaits, same as Onie's. They are so comfortable in this life it seems as though they might have been right here at the Bus Farm all along while the rest of us were growing up somewhere else.

A sign posted in the front says, "Don't say anything unless it's right on." I decide not to say anything. I found out later that they came from LA. Onie had been a fashion designer and striptease instructor, Toby a student at Beverly Hills high school.

"House Truck Al" lives in a bedroom inside the house with his parrot, Gringa. His bus had burnt and now he is building a Victorian house onto the flatbed of an old step van. His room is a mess of sunflower seeds and peanut shells strewn around by Gringa who keeps on squawking "Close the door! Pass the joint! Pass the joint!" This may be Al's way of getting people to share their stash. Wildly bearded, Stan says Al once won a beard-growing contest up in the hills. I stare at the bed of straw stacked inside a weathered wooden frame on the floor where Al apparently sleeps. My eyes wander back to the beard, long and unkempt and overflowing with seeds, stems, and who knows what.

Raison, a diminutive guy with a permanent grin and clubbed feet inhabits an undersized house truck parked next to Al's dismantled van. His high-pitched laugh floats above the farmyard of trucks and buses. Al, Stan, and Raisin carry on about sawzalls and belt sanders; I soak it all in.

I excuse myself to go to the bathroom. Savoring the flush toilet, I sit there reading announcements on the bulletin board. "Skip and Nancy and Les and Kathy announce the births of Elora and Rainbow; Rainbow Gathering, September 1972," somewhere in Montana, according to the card. I wonder about all the people I'm yet to meet. I'm so smitten with the tall guy with the long hair and the dashing mustache I can't think straight. I can't see beyond this moment, nor will I try.

"Oh Stan," Judy had said. "All the girls love him. We call him Sly Stan." A few days later the world froze.

I wake early in my room at the old schoolhouse wrapped tightly in my meager blankets, shivering. The window at the foot of my bed is frozen, covered with arctic-like crackling frost. Traces of my breath float above my head. I lie back down, reluctant to move—make a mental survey of our wood stash. Carol and Kathy are gone—fled to town last night, abandoning their chickens and their goats. Having slept in my clothes, I make a dash for my coat and gloves, slide rubber boots over two pairs of hiking socks and march outside, open the barn door a crack—just enough to squeeze inside and crunch around, offer the animals whatever feed I can find.

Outside, the world is as still as any post-apocalyptic dystopian place, no sounds from the road—not a stir throughout the valley. I'm thinking about bringing the animals inside the house when I hear the clatter of a motor coming up the road. Mary and Tucker moved on weeks ago, and I can't imagine who else might be coming here now, but I recognize the old green truck and watch Stan pull into the driveway, watch him jump out and saunter toward the house, a crumpled bag of groceries clutched to his chest, billows of bitter cold breath flowing in his wake.

When our eyes meet, I think we both know we won't wake up alone and cold tomorrow morning, maybe never again. After we let the chickens into the back porch where they clomp around on their frozen feet, he builds a roaring fire in the rusted woodstove in the kitchen while I slice goat cheese and homemade bread sent by Judy. I take frozen bottles of beer left over from the party onto the porch and set them on the table to thaw. By afternoon we're fed, warm, and full of ourselves. We flirt and laugh and fall for each other in a big way while an ice storm rages outside. Sometime before dark I fall into the wood box and the wall behind the stove begins to smolder. All the water in the place is frozen. Stan grabs an axe and starts pulling apart the kitchen wall while I run around grabbing blankets and pillows to smother what sparks remain inside what's left of the kitchen wall.

By nightfall we're in Stan's bus. In the morning, a sudden rush of intense heat shatters the frozen bus window behind the woodstove. His mustache has turned to ice during the night, and he brushes away dribbles of water as it thaws. Later we go back to the schoolhouse and grab a few of my belongings. I live in the bus now. Simple as that. No discussion. No thought.

After the world thaws, more people in buses, old mail trucks, flatbed trucks, and house trucks show up. They come in hopes of building a dream house on wheels, of becoming players in this growing communal caravan. The farmhouse and its barnyard are a staging area for rolling homes inhabited by craftspeople, musicians, artists, and seekers on the road to an enlightened life, or to Boise, or Seattle, or Nirvana. They call us hippies, but I think we're artists—like the Beats back in the Village, only here there's fir trees and lichen and lots of moss, acres of trees instead of acres of asphalt. At night, lying in our raised bed, we can see headlights out on the interstate drifting past, miles away.

We cut away bus roofs, remove the back ends of step vans; construct Victorian castles on the framework that remains. School bus roofs grow higher—made of wood frame and cedar shakes or welded with more steel to make the interior taller for the gangling young men who live inside. Windows are replaced with stained glass and leaded beveled glasswork— floors are covered with Persian carpeting; upholstery is custom-made with swanky antique fabrics and patchwork leather; we have style. We accumulate antique wood stoves and kitchen stoves at flea markets and antique stores—vintage 19th century.

There is a competition among us—who scored free redwood, who has the strongest engine. It keeps things lively; even when it is muddy and cold, even when things fall apart. If someone needs help, we support each other like any tight-knit

Jonathan's field of house trucks, American Institute of Obnoxious Art. Photo by Jonathan Schwarz

family. Stan is the resident mechanic who works for trades—our bus fills with stained glass lampshades and windows, leather goods, bags of pot, bowls of soup, and homemade breads.

One afternoon, Bret and Mel show up in an old decommissioned postal truck. Bret is a Janis Joplin-like large and loud woman with flaming red hair stringing down her back. I remember her from the deli where I worked during my early days in Eugene. Mel, frail and lost, his one certainty: he is with Bret. They are living in the back of the truck, and they have plans to turn it into a real dwelling, Bus Farm style.

Mel is devoted to Bret, even though she's very pregnant with someone else's baby. She is so pregnant, in fact, she informs us she's in labor. They've come to the Bus Farm to have the baby because, by god, Bret doesn't want to go to no hospital, and Mel isn't going to make her if she don't want to go. Judy and I look at each other. How does Bret think this baby is going to be delivered? But Judy seems complacent and willing to do what's needed. OK then. She says she has some medical books up in the bus, she a former nurse and all. I put some water on to boil for tea. Judy's three-year-old daughter, Aimee, is hanging around the kitchen, and I offer her some leftover spaghetti someone brought for potluck last night.

Judy returns with fresh sheets, herbs, and a midwifery book. We ask Bret if she's sure she doesn't want to go to the hospital over in Cottage Grove. She's sure. She swaggers a little, maybe from the labor, maybe from the draws she's taking on a bottle of Jack Daniels. Been saving it for now, she says. She isn't going to use drugs, but she has to have something for this god-awful pain! The afternoon wears on. Bret gets louder and Judy and I make up a bed in a loft in the spare room. Bret settles under the blankets, kicking and screaming, and as night takes hold, she swears on that bottle of Jack she will never have sex again. I'm hoping Judy knows what she's doing. She's reading the midwifery book aloud as we kneel on either side of Bret. Bret screams. Aimee cries at the door. Mel paces in and out of the room. Bret, you've got to go to the hospital; we all plead. The night erodes, on and on, and at some point, the whisky bottle is empty. I lock eyes with Judy. Someone tells Mel

Building our home on the bus.

to start the truck. Stan and Jack help get Bret out of the bed, down the ladder, and outside into the back of the truck. She collapses or melts into the mattress, and we all sigh as the mail truck speeds off to deliver Bret to medical professionals at the Cottage Grove hospital and impending motherhood.

I ran into Bret one day, years later. She had four kids in tow. "Are these all yours?" I asked, remembering her vow. "They sure are," she replied.

Early that spring, we are evicted—all of us in a state of construction: roofs cut away, piles of lumber and building supplies scattered everywhere. But we pull it together. With our hatches battened, we rattle and roll down the back roads and relocate 20 miles south at our friend Jonathan's country estate. He has dubbed his place the American Institute of Obnoxious Art. The world's largest mother pillow collection on display in his living room, Jonathan adds our ragtag collection of weirdo hippie artists to his installation of American kitsch. He climbs to the bell tower and takes pictures of our parade as we chug down the road toward him, horns honking—house trucks circle up in his muddy spring field.

That summer, we gather around the rickety television set in Jonathan's living room to catch glimpses of the Watergate trial, a reminder of what's going on in the world to which we have turned our backs. Despite our camaraderie, I feel left out of the inner circle—the only one without a baby dressed in Oshkosh coveralls or hand-crocheted ponchos or lacy dresses. Stan and I are the resident aunt and uncle. Aimee asks me one morning when she comes in and catches Stan and I lying on the bed, "Is that your daddy?"

"No, Aimee, that's my sugar daddy." I laugh. She's so cute.

One time a young boy named Sassafras got into his mother's LSD stash. She brought him to us. We stayed up with him 'till dawn, 'till he fell asleep in our arms listening as we read *The Hobbit* aloud while he burrowed safely between us.

But there was something the other women had I couldn't grasp. They seemed so at ease with themselves and their role as hippie moms; I wanted to be part of their sorority even though I had never pictured myself as a mom. The oldest of five, I figured I had changed my share of dirty diapers, sterilized my share of baby bottles, wiped snotty noses, and had felt the kind of responsibility usually reserved for mothers.

Nevertheless, instead of heading downtown one morning on my bike—my usual routine, my way of escaping into my own private world—I made my way through a shroud of dew-covered shrubbery and up a trail to the top of a nearby mountain. Spring wildflowers, Blue Flag iris, violets, and daisies lined the path to the crest of the steep and wooded hillside where a vista of green stretched out until the Oregon foliage collided with a cloudless blue sky and the tips of the Cascade

Mountains—Three Finger Jack and the Sisters and Brothers mountains protruded beyond the skyline.

Late morning sun warmed the top of my head. I wanted to feel the heat against my skin, so I removed my blouse, my long skirt, and my boots. Naked, I raised my arms to the sky, my hair tickling the lower part of my back; I called to my goddess to send me a baby girl—twirled in the sunlight like I had done in the corners of cafes and nightclubs and jazz haunts back east, twirled and danced. I hung around in the small clearing on the top of the little mountain soaking in the sun until it was no longer fierce enough to warm my nakedness. My boots scraped across stones and dirt on the way down.

Along the trail I picked a small bouquet of wild iris. Later that night, I charted a lunar fertility chart—an astrological map identifying the day of possible conception. It would be the upcoming Fourth of July.

I forgot about my plan to go back to New York in a year. Three years had already passed since I made that promise. Iris was born on a sunny spring morning in 1974. About 3:00 a.m. my water broke as I slid out of bed, soaking the floor. Fearing I had wet the bed—my childhood not forgotten—I grabbed my robe and tiptoed across a darkened and sodden field; tiptoed into the house and ran a hot bath in Jonathan's claw-foot tub.

Settling into the steaming water, my head resting on a towel, I closed my eyes and let the warmth soothe my aching back— waited for real contractions. Feeling safe in the early-morning silence of an old house—one man sleeping alone upstairs—I opened the French windows next to the tub. A blanket of misty morning air mixed with the steam of the hot water. Maybe if I stayed right here nothing more would happen, but my uterus began to cramp. I pictured Stan out in the bus, asleep. Maybe he was already up. Maybe he was wondering what became of me, why the bed and the floor were soaked.

He was building a fire when I pulled on the bus door, our rickety wooden door with the beveled glass window kept shut with only a hook and eye. "I think we should call the midwives," I said, smiling up at him from the ground outside.

"It's too early." Did he sound annoyed?

"They must be used to calls at all hours."

He didn't argue and went to the house to use Jonathan's phone. I collected blankets we had sterilized in our propane oven the week before; piled them onto the bed. He must have cleaned the floor and the bed.

A sharp pain forced me up and under the blankets—under the patchwork quilt I'd made on my treadle sewing machine—embroidered a yin-yang sign in the middle and symbols of both of our sun signs, Aries and Leo, one in each corner. By day's end, we'd have another Aries onboard. Our bed frame was taller than my five feet and I had to step from a shelf onto my sewing machine and then heft myself onto the bed. Normal procedure.

Another sharp pain. Where is he? I closed my eyes and drifted; chickens clucked and crowed in a nearby henhouse. The rest of the world was still silent when he put his face close to mine. "They'll be here in about an hour."

"You have bad breath," I said.

He scowled, slouched over to his captain's chair in the corner by the emergency door and strummed his guitar. I was sorry about what I said but said nothing. I wanted to be left alone. Not long after sunup, our gang of three midwives arrived.

I heard people moving about, inside and outside the bus. I floated in my own world, attacked by contractions, one after the other—not much time to rest in between. I rolled over and knelt on the bed letting the load in my belly hang free and ease the pressure on my back. One of the midwives leaned over me with a stethoscope—kind and soft-spoken, one long braid hung over his shoulder and down to his belt. He had this way of inspiring confidence, but on this morning his expression was grim. "I'm not hearing a heartbeat," he says. "We're going to keep an eye on this."

"What?"

"We may have to go to the hospital."

"You're almost completely dilated," said another midwife.

Speaking to Stan who was keeping his distance over in the corner, he said, "We'll have to make a decision soon."

Someone opens the door. "The car is ready."

"You have to put some clothes on."

"No, no clothes. I'll go if I can go like this!"

"You've got to put something on."

Someone puts a robe over my shoulders and some of the Bus Farm guys—David, Logan, and Stan—lift me into the back of Jonathan's Mercedes. The hospital is about a mile away; I lie on the back seat watching treetops whip past overhead as we speed along the winding country road. The sun is up.

The car stops and the door swings open. A gray-haired woman in a nurse's uniform and perky white hat reaches in and spreads my legs. "She's crowning!" she hollers over her shoulder to a bevy of stern-faced, white-capped women. "Get her to the delivery room!"

"Who's your doctor?"

I'm on a gurney, sailing along a cold corridor. "I don't have one."

There is a ruckus going on; something about Stan coming into the delivery room. "Let him in!" I cry out.

People in scrubs move around this hard contraption they've strapped me to. Bright lights. I close my eyes and call for Stan. I won't have this goddamn baby until he's here. He appears next to me in a green hospital shirt.

A young emergency room doc also materializes and is examining me. "I want drugs!"

"Too late for that, young lady. I have to tell you; the baby is posterior."

I sense something, but maybe I'm out of my mind. "What the fuck does that mean?"

". . . turned the wrong way."

"Just give me something for the pain."

"Too late. I'm going to have to cut you, reach in there and pull your baby out. It will be okay . . . here we go".

I am breathing like heck, trying to remember what those Lamaze people said. "Push now; I want you to push!"

I push hard; maybe twice, maybe three times, and Iris Ananda bursts into the world, wailing; I think maybe all three of us are wailing—she, her dad, and I.

Stan's over by this plastic bin where the nurses are washing off the baby. "Give her to me." I watch Stan ease her into his arms while the doctor is stitching me.

They've wrapped her in some kind of bright yellow flannel thing. He comes toward me, holding her, beaming, and places her onto my chest. This is what we've been waiting for. This is the best moment of my life.

"... shaped like an egg ... that blanket. It's almost Easter."
The nurses are chattering around, and before I can take her all
in, the doctor is in my face again.

"Her collarbone is broken ... nothing to worry about; just
a result of the birth ... happens once in a while ... careful
to nurse her on the one side for a while. Just lay her on the
bed next to you for about six weeks, then you can hold her to
nurse."

The old women are shaking their heads. We tell them we
aren't staying, thank you very much—we'll be going back to
the Bus Farm. They fight back, but we're not staying in this
place, and eventually they watch as we depart from the same
emergency room door through which we entered with so much
fanfare not long ago. A gang of house truckers wait for us
in the parking lot. We take off, leaving the doctor and nurses
shaking their heads.

As we pull back into the driveway of the bus farm at the
American Museum of Obnoxious Art, one of those rare full
rainbows hangs over the field behind Jonathan's place, arching
bright prism colors above our trucks and buses. Everyone is
awake.

I lay Iris on the bed, climb up, and take her all in. We look
into her tiny face as though we're examining an alien. Our
hearts are gripped in the sort of love only parents of a baby
less than two hours old can feel. It's the payment for what is to
come, for what must be endured for the rest of your life.

We tell and retell the story of this day for years—the
midwives, the nurses, the rainbow. I wouldn't be surprised if
those nurses have retold the tale a few times.

4

We hit the road a few days later; head up the McKenzie River where we've been offered an entire campground to ourselves, right on the river, a mile or so past the logging town of Blue River. We're about 60 miles east of Eugene at the foot of the McKenzie Pass where chunks of basalt—remnants of ancient volcanos—line the road at the top of the pass.

Our new place is equipped with toilets and showers, and it's far enough away from the highway to be private. Stan parks our rig about 20 feet from the river's edge where we fill bottles

Bus Farm on McKenzie River—Northwest Touring Company. Photo by Roger Beck

Gathering of the clan. Photo by Roger Beck

with drinking water as it races and tumbles by. We eat at picnic tables and hang out at night by our firepits. We ready ourselves for the winter months ahead, work on our crafts, play house. When we aren't working, we swim in secret ice-cold swimming holes up in the hills, trudge up the sides of mountains through almost invisible trails in the national forest to soak in hot springs that only the initiated know how to find.

All these years later, the Cougar Hot springs is a tourist attraction with a parking lot and direction signs.

When the cold weather comes, we gather around crackling stoves long into the night making plans for our caravan adventure. Bus Farm hits the road. We are ready to make our world debut out on the American highways as soon as spring arrives. In the meantime, we live as a communal family by the side of the river—share food, music; dance in the moonlight, cram into handmade sweat lodges made of willow poles and covered in old blankets; roll in the subzero crystalline snow to cool off. Children run from house truck to house truck where women work the stoves, carry babies in slings, grind wheat, bake bread, and stir vats of soups made with organic

NW Touring Company on the road. Photo by Roger Beck

vegetables. Our men hang around campfires passing joints and talking about the state of their engines—which kind of cedar trees make the best shakes, where to get free wood, the price of gas, who will stay, and who will go.

One night I overhear Glenn say something like, "We should get some hotter ladies." Wasn't this a mirror of the patriarchal world we had fought so hard to change in the sixties? Hadn't I sucked up some tear-gas in protest? I keep quiet, but one day I ask Stan why he doesn't fix lunch once in a while.

"Because I change the oil!" A dry wind comes up and I wander away, sit alone on a downed log next to the river, watch it race by.

My long skirt, wet and muddy—my boots are scraped and dirty. I gaze out across the emerald Oregon meadow flourishing the edge of racing mountain waters. I don't know why this doesn't surprise me, but the tall grass and mud fade, and a vast golden desert unfolds. A thunderous parade of camels led by Bedouin-like people clad in dusty silk robes—crimson woven fabrics wrap

59

Lined up for a craft fair. Photo by Roger Beck

their heads—materialize from what is now a desiccated riverbed.
When the dust clears, I see heaps of cargo swaying to and fro on
giant humps of lumbering beasts. Ornate bags hang from the sides
of these magnificent creatures; pottery, beads, and a collection of
trade goods clang and chime as hoofs meet sand. I sit in silence while
the carnival passes. Unaware of my presence, they are engulfed in
a cloud of fine desert powder, I hold my breath; wrap my arms
around my knees—lulled by the music, by the clanging of brass
bells and aromas of incense and spices that have replaced the
heady scent of Douglas Fir and moist river air. At the end of this
bizarre procession, three dwarfs juggling cloth balls dance in the

billowing residue. Strange
and somehow familiar folk,
crowned in turbans and
thick dark braids, march
along expressionless, staring
forward and backward in
time and space. Each strike
of their walking sticks marks
their passage through this
wasteland. Baskets lashed to
their backs appear weightless,

Dickens Faire, 1974.

*for neither they
nor the camels
seem burdened.
A dry wind fills
my nostrils and I
remember the river,
but its pounding
presence is lost to
the future.*

Eastern Oregon.

Jonathan shows up one day in a school bus with the seats
torn out. He has sold the Institute. He couldn't stand being
left behind. House Truck Al arrives in a snowstorm, rumbling
down the dirt road in his Victorian house on wheels, washtub
bass swaying on the back porch of his house truck.

No one wants to be left out. When it's time to go to town,
engines roar, and I take my place next to Iris's port-a-bed
resting on the built-in couch close to the front. I get a chill up
my spine when the engines fire, one by one, and then we begin
to roll, lumbering out onto the McKenzie Highway. You can
see the line of house trucks ahead and behind as each one joins
the procession. I feel a shiver of excitement and the warmth of
belonging.

All the way to town, people along the highway stop and
wave or gawk. Once we reach town, we park in a line in front

of the community store where we stock up on fresh fruits and vegetables, rice, beans, lentils, honey, and tofu. Our homes fill with onlookers and acquaintances wanting to get in on the fun, wanting to check out our scene.

That year we stayed in town during the week before Christmas to take part in the first Dickens Faire, a sort of winter renaissance faire held in an abandoned downtown building—a chance to make real cash to help launch our road caravan in the spring. Stan and I make beaded jewelry, and I have grown a little business selling my patchwork quilts and men's cowboy shirts. We put a hand-painted sign on the side of our bus: Strawberry Patchworks. These cottage industries supported our ambitions. Sam and Pat make leather vests inside their bus opened to the sky through an airplane cockpit. Bonnie sews muslin dresses. Jonathan and Al sell antiques; Blond Bill and Kathy make stained glass windows and lampshades; Roger and Karen sell wire jewelry; Jack and Judy sell and trade Chinese herbs.

When spring finally comes, wildflowers barely in bloom, we head to Boise, Idaho, where we debut our caravan at a craft fair. The plan is to then head east. Iris and I ride up top in the new overhang—her bedroom. Her patchwork curtains sway back and forth, the two of us on our stomachs gazing out over the highway ahead. House trucks loom to the fore, ribboning down the road, up and down and around the Columbia Gorge Highway.

We eat silently late that night—one long table in a local health food restaurant on the edge of Boise. Even the kids are quiet; everyone is ready to climb into their bunks; the rigs are parked out back.

The next day, lined up in downtown Boise, our storefronts open to the public, people throng to get a peek inside, take our pictures, buy a piece of jewelry, leather, or stained glass. They all want to know if we really live in there all the time. Did we make these ourselves? Does that stove really work?

We put donation cans on the dashboards, and they fill with cash—suggested donation 25 cents, but people stuff in greenbacks—one man, a stash of tens and twenties and he says, "This is how much I admire your guts, your hutzpah. You're doing what we all just dream of doing."

But when it comes time to leave, Stan and I are the only ones still pointed eastward. Sam and Pat turn south toward Texas. Everyone else turns their rigs around and head back to the river.

I miss the fields of towering green grasses in the field near my long-ago home on Nine Mile Creek; I miss my mother's macaroni salad, miss the sound of the noon whistle. I miss my aunts and uncles and cousins. I want to go home, so we keep going. Stan has never been east of the Rocky Mountains. We are not going back to the river. We have money in our pockets, and when that is gone, we'll figure something out.

Day two heading east, I ask to drive. Gripping the wheel with both hands, I shift and push the accelerator to the floor. We sail along the interstate, about 50 miles an hour—pots, pans, and glass jars banging and clanging. I maneuver the bus up a steady climb, downshift and listen to the whine of the engine. Our 1950 GMC slows—works harder with each foot of elevation. Eyes fixed on the center of the road, I struggle to hear the engine over the clinking and clanking. I glance in the rearview mirror at a colorful blur of patchwork curtains. Stan sits behind me on the kitchen bench holding Iris, keeping an eye on my driving as we cross the border into Wyoming. The temperature is rising, sweat trickling down my back.

Iris fusses. "Wipe her off with a damp towel," I holler over my shoulder, over the din of the engine.

"My god! Pull over!"

My leg shaking, I pump the brake. "What? What?!"

"Look at the temperature gauge, would you! Don't you watch the gauges when you drive? Are you crazy?!" I ease the bus onto the shoulder of the road, my leg is trembling. The bus lurches to a stop. I put it in neutral, yank on the emergency brake, jump out of the driver's seat and grab Iris in one fluid move.

He is out the door and under the hood. I try to comfort Iris, but she's hot and frightened by the shouting. I slouch back into the driver's seat with her in my arms, ready to hit the brake, to help undo what I've done. We're parked on a steep upgrade in an old school bus with a raised roof and an extended back end. I brush her head and hum a tune about country roads.

He pushes the door open. "Goddamn Onie! He never tightened the motor mount. I knew I should have checked his work! We could have lost the engine!"

By lunchtime it's so hot we decide to leave the highway and follow a narrow two-lane road up into the hills in search of water and a place to spend the night. About a mile up a steep winding byway the pavement ends—the bus sways in the ruts of a thinning dirt road. There is nowhere to turn this giant rig around, so we pursue our only option, forward and upward. Treetops and rough terrain stretch for miles of an uninhabited and endless landscape. Maybe we'll drive all the way to the edge, to the end, no way to turn back. Maybe we'll die, stuck in these mosquito-ridden hills. The engine grinds into granny low.

Are those tears or sweat covering my face? We round a turn and slide onto the smooth surface of paved road, the entrance to a park—a campground with shaded, public bathrooms—heaven. We come to a stop in a parking space out of the sun, sheltered by a row of pine trees. Only a handful of people around—neither of us move or speak for a while.

When the windows are finally down and we're cooled by a delicate cross breeze, I'm the first to get bit. Iris squeaks, too exhausted to cry. Stan slaps his arm and without a word we scamper out of the bus; stand on the sidewalk gasping and scratching. People are staring. The heat rises off the Tarvia. I look around for shade and a place to sit. All eyes are on us. Stan leaps back inside and I hear him banging the windows shut, one by one.

"Better to swelter," he says, loping back down the bus steps.

"We can't sleep in there with no air!" My tears plop onto Iris's bonneted head.

"It's either that or be eaten alive!"

All night long we wash each other and Iris with cool wet rags, fanning her as she sleeps fitfully in her bed at the end of our sleeping loft.

In the morning we're back down the hill at first light, back on the interstate. No longer interested in making breakneck time; when we get to Cheyenne, we do the unthinkable—rent a motel room where we bask in cool showers, eat store-bought sandwiches, and lie on the soft bed.

The next morning, I watch him until he's out of sight. He's gone off on his bike in search of a hardware store. What would it be like if he never came back? Never yelled at me again? I've forgotten who I am, how to defend myself, what I believe about myself and my place in the world. I have an idea that I don't deserve this cruelty I sometimes endure. It reminds me of my childhood in some way.

But he does return a few hours later with a roll of screen and balsam wood and starts right in building screen windows. He is a good guy I think, watching him, watching his intent expression.

When he's finished, we dress Iris in her bonnet and sundress and stroll out by the pool. The air is heavy with heat, the sky brilliant—full of stars bombing past the full moon. The heavens are wider than the mountains are steep. We whisper in our pool chairs about our place next to the McKenzie River. Why have we left home so far behind?

By the time we reach Nebraska, we wear the heat like heavy overcoats, and the highway is an endless quest—a boundless river of farmer's fields enveloped by an unbroken blue sky. Needing a rest and a place to fill our radiator, we take an exit leading down a farm road and pull over. Missy—my fluffy white dog, my loyal pal, sleeping quietly in the back of the bus—runs to the front. A lone car sails past. I open the door and step outside holding Iris on my hip with one arm, shading my eyes with the other. Missy runs past, heading toward a fence where a small herd of cattle eye us with mild interest. She pees and wags her tail. A large black-and-white cow replies with a sharp swoosh of her own tail, an attack on the flies swarming her backside. A stroke of luck—there by the side of the field, next to the cows, sits a galvanized tank filled with water.

"I don't think these girls will mind if we borrow some of this, do you?" Stan is unscrewing an empty water jug and smiling at me for the first time in days. I smile back. This will come in handy if the bus overheats. There's a breeze. Missy rolls in the grass. It's quiet here on this Nebraskan byway— only the muffled sound of the nearby interstate. We eat our lunch of leftover rice and salad I've saved in our antique oak icebox. Afterward, we walk up and down the road.

"We better make time; find a place to park for the night." I nod in agreement and flit around the bus, make sure everything is put away, tied down. Iris has fallen asleep.

Our house tips and groans as it lumbers onto the road. "I think we can merge with the interstate if we go straight ahead," I say, examining the map.

The interstate flows along a constant pattern of brown and green. We've gone 50 miles, and I take out the map again. "Let's stop someplace where Missy can have a nice run and maybe sit in some water—maybe a little creek; she'd like that." I look at Stan for approval.

He's looking at me in the rearview mirror. He looks back at the road and then swirls back around, glaring at me now, then back at the road, and then back at me. "Where the hell is that dog?!"

I run to the back, lift covers and pillows; look under the bed. " . . . she's not here!"

"Oh great. That goddamn dog! We're not going all the way back. She can just stay in that field!"

"No way! We've got to go back!" Iris is awake and crying. I pick her up and kiss her. We veer off an exit, and I cling to the kitchen counter with one hand and Iris with the other. The bus pitches. He guns the engine.

We are heading back the way we came in silence, not a word. Please God, let Missy be there with the cows. She must be scared and confused. Maybe she wandered off looking for us. How long have we been gone? I'm not sure. In my life, all my praying has been for dogs, my dogs—my secret efforts to keep them safe.

The cows are still gathered around the water tank. They look up as though to say, "Back so soon?" Stan kills the engine. Am I next? I don't see Missy. He is out the door, and I gather Iris in my arms.

"You idiot dog! You stupid dog!"

I round the front of the bus. Missy's head is hung low, covered in cow dung. "You're going to clean her up before she gets in that bus!"

"I will. I will." I hand Iris over and hurry back inside in search of a rag and a towel, maybe a bucket and some soap. My long skirt drags and catches on the tall grass. "Stay there, Missy."

I dip a bucket into the lukewarm liquid in the galvanized tank filled with dead flies, bits of hay, and debris. Poor Missy. Her big brown eyes say it all. I'm so embarrassed. She must have tried to sidle up to the cows when she realized she was alone, and they must have given her a shower. Poor Missy. Come here girl. I rinse her in hopes of removing the worst of the shit from her soft white coat. She stands still, her head nearly touching the ground. I repeat the process until her Poodle-Terrier locks droop with the weight of the water and

the cow dung. Then I wash her down with soap. Stay. I trudge
through the tall grass to borrow more water from the cows.
Missy waits for me to return, to rinse the rest of the soap from
her fur. This crisis is almost over.

It's been a long ride. We are resting on the banks of the Platte
River. Two Sandhill Cranes, silent as stone, also grab a break
on the river's edge. They watch us from a safe distance on
the other side of the coffee-colored waters. Two young boys
playing near the water's edge squeal and splash and fill their
plastic buckets with dark wet sand, then dump the damp
mess onto each other's feet. Without warning, the large white
birds spread their wings in unison; lift their bulk with ease
into the vast Nebraskan sky. Stan and Iris sit together, quietly
examining a flat, wet stone. Father and daughter.

Grateful for a break from the baby I'm still not used to, I
focus on myself for a few precious moments, the ache in the
center of my chest. I'll be home soon, home for the first time
in years.

The last tethers have worked their way loose, and for a long
time I have felt no urge to go back. Now I long to be there. I
can hardly wait another hour, but with the kind of time we're
making it will be at least two days. Watching and feeling the
sure current of this slow-moving river, I measure our time
from rock to rock, city to city, breast feeding to breast feeding.

As the afternoon slips away, we make good time—sail
our prairie schooner across Iowa. Cornfields replace dreary
Nebraskan wheat fields, and though it's still unbearably hot,
there are more places here to find shelter from the sun. At
lunchtime we rumble into a rest area somewhere in the middle

of an ocean of farmland and lurch to a stop in the only sliver of shade for miles. Our benefactor, a broad-leafed oak tree, stretches its branches toward the noon sun. Once the engine is exhausted, we run up and down the bus, lowering each window with a clang. The cross-breeze is shallow, but we appreciate each tiny whiff of countryside and its deafening silence after the constant noise of the highway.

Stan is already outside checking out our temporary backyard. I see him lean against the trunk of the tree and stretch his legs. Despite the heat and her hunger, Iris is singing a loud song in her own language, banging a wooden spoon on the tray of her antique oak highchair.

Maybe it's the racket we're making inside the bus, but I haven't heard the truck pull up. Outside my kitchen window there's a red pickup truck and two men talking to Stan. I can't make out the conversation, but two shotguns hanging in the rear-window gun rack catch my eye.

Crouched behind the curtain, I hear them ask Stan if maybe he doesn't need a haircut, Boy. They will be glad to oblige. One of them lets out a hoot, and I know for certain we are in trouble.

Before Iris can make another sound, I have her out of the highchair. She wears nothing but a diaper and a white islet bonnet. I don't have time to think straight, and even if I did, I know I must act on instinct. They both see me at the same time and stop in mid-sentence, or mid-guffaw, like a freeze-frame movie clip. I too remain frozen inside the doorway, locked in a stare down with these two rednecks.

As though someone has released a gummed-up reel on a 16-millimeter projector, the action starts up once more. But I do not move. I know I must be a sight to behold standing in my kitchen door in the middle of a cornfield, holding my baby, my long skirt swirling in a sudden prairie breeze. I keep my eyes wide and unblinking, and when these men see they haven't scared me, they are again deflated.

"You're not going to hurt us, are you?" I come right out and ask the obvious, knowing that if either of us runs, mentally or physically, they will chase us like wild dogs.

When the eternal minute has finally passed, they look at each other and drag their dusty boots on their way back to the jacked-up pickup. The shorter one, the one in the cowboy hat and the tight jeans, hops up into the driver's seat and guns the engine. The other one, older and meaner looking, runs his hands through his slicked back hair and then adjusts his rolled-up sleeves around well-tended biceps. He considers the possibilities, looks over at Stan who has not moved this whole time, then pulls himself up into the truck and shuts the door.

Neither of us budge or breathe as the back end of the red pickup truck disappears into a cloud of prairie dust.

5

When we arrived in Syracuse, the local paper did a feature on us and our home.

Artsy Craftsy Bus-home Travels across the Country

Syracuse Herald American, Aug. 25, 1974, article by Carolyn Straub
It looks like a barn on wheels. It was once an old school bus. Now it's a home, a crafts studio and a means of transportation.

"I cut off the original roof with a cold chisel and split the wood myself," says originator Stanley Hayworth. And the bus became "Strawberry Patchworks," a house and a career on wheels!

"We just have fun creating things, making everything around us beautiful!" say occupants of the "house truck," Stan and his wife, Nancy, of Eugene, Oregon. The home is also a crafts bus and is filled with needlecraft.

The pair recently traveled cross country with small daughter Iris Ananda (Ananda is Sanskrit for "bliss") and shaggy dog, "Missy," to exhibit their handiwork in crafts fairs in the Central New York area.

"People wave and smile in the streets when we pass," smiles Nancy who notes her only dislike for the life "is that it's sometimes hard to find a parking space!"

The 26-year-old couple have been visiting Nancy's parents, Mr. and Mrs. Peter W. Cole of Marcellus, and plan to exhibit handwork

Parked in my parents' backyard, Upstate New York. Syracuse Herald American
today in the 'Women Are Many Faces' festival, Everson Museum of
Art, and 'Superfair' Tuesday through Saturday.

Skaneateles and Canandaigua crafts fairs have already seen
their talents as well as others. The Hayworths plan their return
trip in early September.

It all began when Nancy and Stan met on a 'bus farm' in
Oregon where a group of friends were building 'craft buses.'

The inside of our bus home. Syracuse Herald American

The Hayworth's reflects a simple life, perhaps after Early America. It looks, on the interior, like an old log cabin with bed tucked cozily in the rear. All around are patchwork quilts, a patterned carpet.

Smells are of forest wood, Hemlock, cedar and Douglas fir woods went into the shaping of Stan's "unique design." A mechanic, he also fashioned the barn-type door, installed leaded windows and painted the finished creation an earthen brown.

"Everybody likes it!" says Nancy. "We use kerosene lamps, no electricity, and an old style 'airtight,' a wood stove."

A friend crafted a stained-glass window in a daffodil design for the Hayworth 'home.' Nancy credits her crafts interest to her grandmother, the late Mrs. Grace Parsons Cole, an art instructor at Marcellus in the early 1900s and a greeting card designer.

Among domestic arts, the young craftswoman enjoys quilting and sews most of the family's clothing using a treadle machine.

One of her curtains is a crewel work flower design. Embroidery, knitting, crocheting are more hand done enjoyments.

Her husband is a native of The Dalles, Oregon, end of the Oregon Trail.

We stay in my parent's backyard all summer, except for the times we're at craft fairs or even, for one week, parked at the end of the midway, just outside the Dairy Building, at the New York State Fair. We are freaks, a novelty. People want to get a look.

My friends from school don't come by. Mom's potato salad has lost its flavor. I load Iris into the stroller someone brought over and take off to find the old town, down Main Street, soaking it all in. Everything has changed. The hardware store is now a pizza parlor. Thomas's Five and Dime is a realty office. Also gone, the movie house, the soda fountain, and the gift shop. They rebuilt the post office and there's a hair salon where I used to collect our mail from the nice lady behind the barred window. Coe's meat market is boarded up—the little grocery on the corner where we used to get apples for a nickel. People pass on the sidewalk—no one I recognize. Down at the mill, there's nothing left but a falling down building, bricks piled haphazardly next to a boarded-up front door.

"Do you want to see the swans?" I ask Iris. I push her out behind the abandoned woolen mill where my grandmother and I once collected scraps for braided rugs, where we dug through gigantic bins while rackety looms wove the wool amid the hum of the machinery. I hear the spray of the waterfall before we reach the edge of a cement embankment. No swans, just an empty soda carton floating on the surface of the pool below the falls.

Great Aunt Martha comes to visit one day. She looks around the bus, fingers the handle on the 1930s propane stove, the globe on the kerosene lantern. She looks at me and says, "You know, we were so happy when we finally got electricity, we could hardly believe the convenience of being able to walk into a room and switch on a light, cook and heat the house without having to chop wood and build a fire." She smiles and pats me on the back.

My father and Stan keep up a thinly veiled effort to get along. He and my younger sister Melissa fight at the dinner table. "That kid's a 14-year-old brat! She would have gotten one upside the head if she'd lived at my house." It's time to go.

On the morning of our departure the bus is parked out front. Neighbors come out to wave goodbye. Aunt Helen and Uncle David come to see us off. My father appears, carrying a 50-pound bag of potatoes. "Put these under your bed," he says. I see the tears in the corners of his eyes but pretend not to notice. "They might come in handy."

Stan waits for me inside the bus; Missy is on the floor next to him. We are going home. We pull away from my parents' house and meander through the town from whence I fled nearly five years ago. I stare out the window until we reach the outskirts of town. I am trying to imprint the images of a village.

6

Breezing along the southern tier of New York State and then bouncing along the Pennsylvania Turnpike, we sing above the roar of the engine. Tires whir. Take me home! Country roads, to the place, I beloooong . . .

Day two, we're heading in a southerly direction down the mountain passes of Virginia—going home, but still breathing the air of places we've never been and will probably never be again. Our house carries us up and down and around an endless mountain highway, green as far as you can see.

It's early morning. Sunday. The fresh air in these foothills fills us with enthusiasm for the long trip back. Once we turn westward, we'll stop in Nashville and rest for a few days. *Blue Ridge Mountains, West Virginia! Take me home . . . "*

Why is Stan pumping the brakes? He keeps downshifting, one gear and then the next. I cease my reverie and creep to the front of the bus, hang on to the back of his seat. "We've lost our brakes!"

I've come to trust his ability to get us out of situations in one piece. I keep my cool. We're bearing down a long steep hill. Early Sunday morning, there are no cars on the road. "Hold on to Iris!"

I trip, try to grab a post by the woodstove, but as though in an ocean torrent, the bus picks up speed and I fall to the floor next to Iris's porta-bed. I heave her down onto my lap and try to make a game out of what now feels more and more desperate. "Mountain mama . . ." I sing into her soft baby ear, wrap my arms around her tiny body as we bump along on the floor. I watch Stan working the clutch and the gear shift, double clutching, sounding the horn. Cast iron frying pans and kitchen pots sway back and forth—a crescendo of metal and glass drown out the roaring and the screeching.

"I'm going to try and pull off into a parking lot up ahead!" he hollers, and in seconds—that feel like hours—we creak to a stop in the deserted parking lot of an auto repair shop—not a car or a person in sight, only an abandoned truck held aloft by four cement blocks over by the edge of a spindly wooded area.

"Looks like we'll be here until they open in the morning." He is still hugging the wheel. I'm still hugging Iris.

We are alive. We have a place to park, right? Neither of us is sure about anything.

A few days later, we're back on the road—brakes fixed, enthusiasm damaged, but the sight of a pink morning sky over Knoxville silhouetting high-rise buildings that loom in the distance is a reminder we are on the road again. Mountain passes behind us, we're heading due west. Cars pass like ghosts on the highway. We ride in quiet stillness. We'll eat when we get to Nashville.

When he edges our rig into several adjacent and empty parking spaces in the Nashville university district and cuts the engine, we sigh, but before we can stand, there's a pounding on the door—a crowd outside lined up on the sidewalk. Stan opens the door.

"We'd like ta take a look at yawl's bus."

Stan looks at me; I nod, and in less than a beat our house is filled with gawkers.

"Did you build this yourself?"

"Where ya'll from?"

"Do you live in here all the time?"

"Does that stove really work?" We answer all the questions. We've heard them all before, and I discretely push the donation can toward the door.

It's quiet again as the last curious soul steps down onto the curb. Stan latches the hook on the door and takes a final peek through the window. Before he can turn around there's another knock. He opens the door. A woman peeks over the back of the stairwell, almost pushing him back into the driver's seat. "Sorry for the intrusion." I'm trying to look enthused.

"I own a boutique just up the street?" She points to something, and I smile and nod. "Well, I just got a call from someone at one of the Nashville TV stations. They heard about you and would like to come out and interview you for the five o'clock news. Would that be OK?"

"Sure." We are mentally adding up potential donations; the can is now permanently in place by the front door. "Sure."

The news crew arrives a couple hours later laden with giant television cameras and microphones. Iris is in her highchair, ready for

Iris entertains gawkers in Nashville.

dinner, kicking her legs while I spoon smashed bananas and pears into her eager mouth. They point their cameras at us and ask all the same questions. They film me feeding the baby. They film the inside of the bus and the outside of the bus. They want to know how we got involved with this lifestyle. Are we happy? Are we heading home?

After they're gone, two medical students from Vanderbilt University invite us to park in their backyard for the evening to watch the piece on the news and to stay for a few days.

We follow Randy and John through winding neighborhood streets. Once we're settled in their driveway, they run to our door and invite us inside. We share stories about our lives over dinner. These two are in med school, on the highway to career success. We'll be lucky to make it to Oregon in one piece.

Randy is about 30—short hair. He's wearing a crisp pinstriped shirt. There's a genuineness about him I'm not used to. He asks if he can hold Iris. While he's cuddling her, I catch him looking at me. What's he's thinking? Probably that I'm pretty and smart and what the heck am I doing with my life in that bus.

Memphis by morning. Smitten with Nashville hospitality, we're reluctant to leave, but we've been here for days and it's time to move on. The highway and the river beckon. We decide to leave during the night while traffic is light and the air cool. We drift into Memphis by way of an industrial parkway; wander side streets lined with warehouses.

Stopped at a traffic light, I gaze out the window—people are hustling down the sidewalk on their way to work. They are living lives I'll never know about in this city I'll never see again. They are fixed, and we are aimless.

"Are those guys honking at us?"

"I don't know."

"I think you should pull over."

The light turns green, and we cross the intersection and park next to the curb. Before either of us is out of our seat, they're knocking on the door.

"Man! This is something else! Where're y'all headed?" Two guys with long hair and patched jeans are trying to get a look in my kitchen window.

"Do you need a place to park this here rig? Yer welcome to put her in our backyard." I try to catch Stan's eye—No! I want to make time. I want to go home.

"We're havin' a cookout tonight!" At least these backyard campgrounds come with dinner, a shower, and a toilet. "Follow us!" one of them yells from the front window of their dusty station wagon.

Bumping along the back streets of downtown Memphis, I remember our expired license plates and what might be the consequence if we get pulled over. We don't have enough money to renew the plates at the rate of one-hundred dollars and make it home; we've already passed several cop cars and state police, but they too seem more intent on gawking at the bus than noticing our misdemeanors.

I cozy my feet up to the crackling campfire, sip homemade beer. We tell them about the brakes failing coming down the mountain pass in Virginia, about life on the Oregon river that runs ice cold down the Cascade Mountains—a ribbon of

Douglas fir trees separating God's world from the McKenzie Highway jammed with rapids of overflowing log trucks.

The tall lanky guy with a long blond ponytail says, "Y'all can't come to Memphis and not visit Graceland!"

Stan brightens and pours himself another glassful of beer. But I'm thinking about bed, about the strength we'll need to put thousands of miles behind us before we'll hear the music of our beloved river again.

We sleep the sleep of the dead-tired, and in the early morning over cups of coffee and a burned-out campfire we make plans.

"It's so early. Can't we just hit the highway?" Stan is not listening to me. They're giving him directions to Elvis's place.

"Heck. Just follow us. We'll lead you on up there." No way out of this.

Their station wagon bounces down a long potholed drive and the bus tilts and banks as we pull out onto the street filled with morning traffic. We've wasted at least an hour. I peer out the window over the side of the bridge. The Mississippi River looks as though it has stopped in its tracks.

They guide us through traffic; point us toward the road to Graceland, to Elvis. We exit the parkway where they've told us to follow the hill to the top. "You can't miss the mansion!" They are enthusiastic about sending us up to meet their King.

I'm aware of the rumbling noises we make—jars clanging, the bus itself creaking and groaning, more so when we hit a bump in the driveway pulling up to the entrance of Graceland, like bums at the gate. Will they shoo us away? Maybe yell at us for trespassing? It's early morning; I don't see anybody. The gate is wide open. Oh well. Stan cuts it off, and here we are.

"Now what?"

"I don't know," I say. "Should we get out? Ya think he'll come out here?"

A small chunky guy with slicked back black hair is coming down the drive. "Shit"

"Howdy. Some rig y'all got here." Buddy hops up our stairwell and hangs in our doorway. "Hope you don't mind if I come on in?"

"No, not at all. We hope we're not trespassing, or . . . ?"

"Not'all. Too bad Elvis's outa town. Geez, he sure woulda liked to see this here house on wheels . . . is that what it is?"

"Yes." Stan jumps at the chance to talk about how he cut the roof off the bus with a sawzall and built the raised roof out of lumber with handmade joists; how he cut off the back end, extended it, squared it off to make our bedroom, and finished it with precious redwood siding. "I installed a door at the bottom so we can load supplies under the bed from the outside."

"That's something. So y'all're makin' yer way around the country?" We nod and I wait for the questions, but he seems satisfied imagining who we are and what we are doing. "I'll be darned; if that don't beat all."

I ask if he'd like a cup of tea, but Buddy says he has to get into Memphis. He shakes both our hands, gives me a hug, but stays on the bus as we circle past the front of Graceland, a house too big to be a home I contemplate.

He's still waving as we circle one more time. He waves and hollers loud enough for us to hear, "Take care now. I'll be sure to tell Elvis you was here."

The MacPherson boys

We made arrangements before we left New York to stop in Albuquerque to visit my mother's brother, Johnny, and then to stop in Riverside, California, to visit one of her other brothers, Dick, and his large tribe of kids and grandkids. I had never met these relatives before. The truth is, I don't know my mother's side of the family, only the stories she's told and retold about when they were kids in International Falls.

I felt that I knew each one of them, knew what they would be like. I knew all about their life, how they had outshined all the other boys up there in the frozen North Country—the MacPherson boys. They were talented skiers, loggers, dancers; they were handsome and brave. They got in fights. They got in and out of trouble like Butch Cassidy and the Sundance Kid— superheroes of my mother's imagination. I couldn't wait to see them in the flesh.

Johnny and his wife Betty live in a condo on the outskirts of Albuquerque that looks out across a vast flat land that ends abruptly at our first sighting of the foothills of the Sierra Nevada's—an entryway to the western country we hope to reach soon. They meet us at the door and seem genuinely thrilled to meet us. Johnny actually does look like Paul Newman, dark curly hair, chiseled jawline, ice blue eyes—the same as mine. I can't stop looking at him.

We sit in the living room chatting with Betty while Johnny is in the kitchen making us a surprise dinner, something he remembers had been my mother's favorite dish. I can't wait. I am starving and I know Stan is too. Iris knocks over a couple of Betty's knick-knacks, nearly breaking them, but she is matter of fact about it, putting them up on a higher shelf. "We don't have any grandchildren yet," she smiles. "I wish my sons, Pat and Mike, were in town. They would love to meet you, and I know they'd love to see your bus."

Johnny calls from the dining room. The table is set beautifully. I can smell something that I can't quite recognize. Smells good I say and wait to see what the surprise dish is. Betty passes a serving dish, piled high with what looks to be a root vegetable of some kind, sort of like white carrots. "Oh, wow," I say. Oh my god, I think.

"I know how much your mother loved parsnips," Johnny smiles, pleased. He watches as I pile two or three on my plate. I don't dare look at Stan. I search the table for butter, but don't see any. My uncle is waiting for me to taste this delicacy. If my mother loved these so much, I think, I wonder why I have never heard of a parsnip. I slice the vegetable into a bite-sized pieces, smiling as they enter my mouth and I bite down. The message shoots quickly from my tongue to my brain. It isn't favorable—bitter and tasteless. At what point in her life had this been my mother's idea of delicacy? I will survive this dinner. It isn't so bad I can't eat it. How sweet that this man has remembered something about his and my mother's childhood—probably a Depression nightmare.

After dinner, we pile in the back seat of their Cadillac convertible and cruise the neighborhoods of Albuquerque. They want to show us Old Town. We drive past Johnny's car lot. I feel safe and relaxed for the first time in days in the backseat of this stranger's car, the stranger with familiar eyes.

It's funny, I think later as I'm lying in bed watching the headlights on the distant highway heading up into the hills, that there is this whole part of my family I've never met. I'm like a chocolate chip cookie, without all its chips.

My heart aches for Oregon. For now, it seems more doubtful every day we will make it. The interstate across Arkansas and Texas is terminal, monochromatic, endlessness. "Where are all the cowboys?" I wonder aloud late one afternoon.

"I don't know, and I don't care." I can see that he is tired. Iris has been fussy all day, and I've done my best to keep them both from going overboard, from dying of hopelessness and lack of good air.

A few days later in California, I am shocked to meet more relatives who are more than strange. People I would not talk to on the street. We have stumbled into a house filled with an extended family that keeps dishes in the dishwasher to keep the roaches off—can't use the pool because it is filled with floating objects and old diapers. We are stuck in front of their house. We have run out of money and now forced to use our ingenuity to get out of here, forced to get to know these people with the ice blue eyes who aren't so bad once you get to know them. They don't offer to help, but we finally sell some of our wares—beaded jewelry—and hightail it out of San Bernardino.

By the time we're heading north out of Bakersfield, we've replaced our clutch in Mussel Shoals, Alabama, taken the front off someone's car in a parking lot in Arkansas—the second and last time I was allowed to drive; we've driven through wind-stripped prairies and snow-packed mountain passes. Somehow, we bore the blazing heat in the Mojave Desert. The idea of air conditioning is unheard of. We keep our eyes out for cops and rednecks. We fight. Once he leaves me in the parking lot at a rest stop. I have no money and no coat, just a baby to breastfeed. I sit quietly on a bench waiting for the next thing to happen. The next thing is the sight of my house returning. "Get in," he says. I have no choice.

We pass John Deere tractors pulling trailers loaded with boxes of grapes, dark-skinned people walking slowly along the side of the road carrying sacks on their way to or from work. The landscape is big and flat, a world I know nothing about. The blistering heat is dryer than I've ever felt. I want to be gone. I want to be in Oregon where the air is light, where rich green blankets cover the hillsides.

We disappear into a mantle of fog. You can barely see the next car. We've made peace, the two of us—head north in the kind of silence that exists between people who no longer care enough to fight. I-5 North is the final setting for our seemingly endless march toward our seemingly unreachable goal. But we're determined to cross the border into Oregon before the night is over. Heading into the mountains in northern California, we see the first signs of Ponderosa Pine and Douglas fir trees. We're almost home.

We push on. Iris fusses. She and I sleep. Stan drives the bus. Nighttime is catching up and we follow the pass upward into the Siskiyou Mountains. We'll spend the night in Ashland once we've crossed into Oregon. A final shred of daylight; roiling thunderclouds. The bus strains, grinding upward to 4,000

On the banks of the McKenzie. Photo by Roger Beck

feet. It starts to snow. I see into the growing darkness through clacking windshield wipers. As we begin our descent, the bus picks up speed. Downshift. It's freezing cold, but I'm sweating. Downshift. Tractor trailers roar past. The road is slick, and I know our tires are worn. Please God, don't let us come this far and die now. The night is starless, but the sky is filled with a crazy quilt of enormous snowflakes. I struggle not to cry. I know he is exhausted and as unsure of the outcome as I.

Once we make it all the way to our old spot by the McKenzie River, we stay there on the bank until winter. We fight about who's supposed to fix lunch, where I've been all afternoon, when we're going to town, and why I don't want him to touch me. There have been days I run for my life, clutching Iris in my arms. Our fairy tale life in our make-believe house is falling apart faster than wet gingerbread. Unlike fixing brakes and clutches and motor mounts, we have no tools to fix this. It's time to go.

The end of an era.

7

I am a single mom, a college student, and a soul mate detective. I'm picking up where I left off with my college career. The strike was a class suicide of sorts, one of my friends called it. We had taken a stand against the war; how could that be a bad thing? I have decided I want to be a social studies teacher. I want to tell young people about what happens when first-world countries try to colonize third-world countries in the name of freedom—about greed, about death, about ruin. I want to tell them about the My Lai massacre where American soldiers brutally killed most of the people—women, children and old men—in the village of My Lai on March 16, 1968; about the death of tens of thousands of my peers, about the gunning down of innocent college students at Kent State on May 4, 1970; about the alienation of an entire generation for the country to which they pledged allegiance every morning of their childhoods. Iris turns three this year, and I've enrolled her in day care—our first time apart.

I love my '53 Cadillac coupe—Dagmars jut from the front grill like bombshells; a winged-bird hood ornament guides me along the byways of my new and uncertain life. The fire is my fault.

I get to the side of the road before the car stops running altogether. Having lived all those years with a mechanic, handing him tools and watching over his shoulder listening

Iris and me. Photo by Jonathan Schwarz

to grease monkey lingo, I am practically a mechanic myself, right? I get out of the car and heave the monstrous hood; examine the maze of wires and hoses, and my eyes rest on the carburetor. I know it's a carburetor. Yes. I'll take that apart and clean it.

I don't notice that the little glass bubble is filled with gasoline. I remove it, not seeing or smelling the gas spilling everywhere. It's nighttime. I wipe it clean, careful to strip out every speck of dirt and debris and then replace the gasket and its cover and jump back into the car—hood still hovering in the air beneath the streetlamp—to give it another try. I have to get home.

Flames shoot 20 feet in the air. I have only seconds to escape. The fire rages. Neighborhood people run from their houses to see what's going on, to watch with me in silence as firemen douse what's left of my Caddy. The man who called the fire department offers to give me a ride home. It had been the starter that was the problem, and it sparked when I tried to start the engine covered in gasoline. The next day the charred wreckage was towed away, and I never saw that car again.

Iris and I move into a friend's house while they're in Mexico for the winter. It's close to the university, close to Iris's preschool. Stan comes occasionally and takes her for the weekend. We may have loved each other, but we can't retrieve what's lost.

One day after he's dropped her off and he's pulling out of the driveway, Iris puts her forehead to the front window, presses her face against the large glass pane, and cries in the way that breaks a mother's heart. Later I wipe the dried snot and tears off the window. I can still picture her crying after her dad, and my heart still breaks at the thought of it.

I may have escaped a life on the road, but not Stan. Sometimes I'll be driving down some side street, look in the rearview mirror, and there he is, on my tail. The other night he broke into the house and charged into my bedroom to see who might be there. Not long ago when my mother was visiting, he came after me with an axe. She was so terrified she jumped on a city bus, found her way to the airport, and flew home that day—angry at me for putting myself and Iris in this situation.

I don't know what to do. If I go back to New York, Iris will want her dad and someday, and in her mind, it will be my fault for taking her away from him. I'm homesick, I am, but no matter what, I don't think it's the right thing to leave. I need a plan—the restraining order isn't working.

My friends and my brother, Peter—who followed me to Oregon a couple years ago and built a house bus like his older sister's—and I organized my escape. He rented a cabin for me—sight-unseen on my part—in a remote area of southern Oregon—a trailer attached to a cabin, a ramshackle place atop a lonely hill on about three acres overlooking the Elkhead Valley. There's a dilapidated sign on the side of the road winding through Scott's Valley, Welcome to Elkhead. But that's it. No indication of a town or even a four-corner stop. Rusted barbed wire holds up falling and crumbling old fence posts covered in blackberry brambles. My driveway is the last turn-off before the road to the old Langdon place, remnants of a quicksilver mine.

Peter and his friends and my friends came to my house in town in the middle of the night. Like robbers, we hurried to load my belongings into his bus, remove all traces of me from the house where Iris and I lived, where lately I'd been living in fear of Stan showing up in the middle of the night. When we were finished loading the bus with boxes and a few pieces of furniture, I hugged my friend Kathy goodbye. I followed Peter down the freeway, Iris asleep in the back seat—fleeing one life, on my way toward a shadowy new life—an inmate escaping across a raging river to safety.

Sometimes, after Iris is asleep at night, I sit in the bone-chilling stillness beneath the crystal-clear sky bowl in this remote countryside and cry like a she-wolf who has lost her den. I know my dreams of a family in the patchwork cabin in the old school bus are not going to work out. Someone is going to get hurt. One night I dream that I'm running down the side of the road, chasing the bus, trying to get back in—trying to get my home and my life back.

When love breaks, so does the heart—sometimes more than that. The idea of a broken heart is merely an image to help explain the real pain in the center of the chest. We do whatever we can to alleviate the wrenching, the confusion. It's nerve-wracking, but it can also lead you toward a new understanding of yourself and life in general—sometimes a test of the lines between sanity and insanity.

Either way, for the first time in years, I feel safe. He won't find me here in this place on the top of the hill, but I keep an eye on the long winding driveway just in case. There's plenty to do to keep busy. I've planted a massive vegetable garden with the help of a farmer's son who lives up the road. I trade him a handmade cowboy shirt for plowing the fenced-in flat land at the bottom of the hill next to the creek. I put in potatoes, rows of corn, eggplant, tomatoes, and herbs.

Yesterday Iris and I drove 20 miles to the nearest town in search of supplies at the dusty little feed store where it smells like cow manure and rancid gasoline. I filled the trunk of my car with bales of straw, a roll of clear plastic, and a set of child-size garden tools. Iris is happy when she's helping, and at three years old she's a burgeoning gardener and digs behind me with her new rake, shovel, and hoe. There's no phone here. Our bathroom is an outhouse out back—up the hill. We have one neighbor, Ted.

A scruffily bearded man, Ted always wears the same Army surplus jacket. He's minding the neighbor's pot patch while they're living in LA making a go of it in the comedy circuit. Iris and I walk across the field and through a break in the fence to get to his backyard where I often find him tinkering in the barn or weeding the vegetable garden. He's helpful and friendly, sharing gardening tips and often rallying to help the mysterious woman with the three-year-old girl. He's offered to teach me how to grow pot. ". . . a sure-fire cash crop," he says, scratching at his knee through the hole in his worn-out jeans. Ted keeps to himself, keeps the gate at the bottom of his driveway shut and locked.

I'm putting stock in my cowboy shirt business. The other day I snuck into Eugene—kept to the back streets—bought bolts of muslin at the fabric shop. Iris helped collect textile scraps for patchwork finishings and trims at the Goodwill As-Is store. Ted has deconstructed his precious gate and made a booth out of the lodge poles so I can sell shirts at the Renaissance Faire. Sometimes he and I sit on his rambling front porch at night, watch the sun set, talk about fertilizer, about how fucked up things are in the world beyond our hidden retreat.

I follow the moonlit path back across the field to my cabin—crystalline stars wink in the night sky amid a chorus of crickets. In some ancient cultures, the cricket's song represents a signal for the coming of a fortunate life.

Last week Iris and I drove to the coast and filled the car trunk with white beach sand. When we got home, I backed up close to the two by six sandbox frame I'd hammered together—we shoveled the sand into the box. I watched Iris digging with her shovel, looked down at the top of her determined head of soft-brown hair.

Later that summer my mother came for another visit. She walked in the front door and surveyed the plywood-covered living room floor draped end to end with yards and yards of white muslin. I was cutting out dresses and shirts, getting ready to sew them together and build up my stock of one-of-a-kind shirts and dresses for the Renaissance Faire—now called the Oregon Country Fair. This is a chance to make some money so Iris and I can survive the winter. Who knew how many times my car would make it up and down the steep winding country road once the rain and mud took hold?

I thought my mother would be impressed with my resourcefulness and my independence. But it's not unusual to have expectations of someone they simply cannot fulfill. Once again, she's furious; says she's ashamed of her daughter living in squalor.

Regret, I've come to understand, is a homeless emotion. It takes up residence in the heart like a hobo under a bridge. Sometimes I regret leaving home, all the times I left home, all the empty hours I've wasted when I could have been painting or walking in the woods; I regret not loving honestly, not loving enough, loving too much; I regret losing the debris of life that disappears through neglect and chaos; I regret not paying attention, the passing of time, the loss of love, the loss of days gone by.

We make decisions that change our lives forever—leave our homeland for an unknown place, take up with strangers, take up a new life and a new lifestyle. We are pilgrims, explorers, pioneers, trailblazers, adventurers, and wanderers. We make mistakes. And why should we regret the blessing of a hard-learned lesson? We are either lost or in the vanguard. When I left New York for Oregon, I believed I would go back home one day. But one day led to another—to a new person, to a new place, a new homeland—one leads to another until I'm lost in a maze of my own making. Some call it fate; some call it free will. That's an existential debate that has not been settled.

The poet and songster, Patti Smith, wrote in one of her memoirs: "Some things are not lost but sacrificed." Did I zig when I should have zagged, or did I get it exactly right? Winter is coming on. My dirt and gravel driveway, slick and muddy; my wheels spin, gravel flies—sometimes we leave the car and climb the hill to the cabin, hauling wet grocery bags in the rain.

Stan found me last week. I grabbed Iris when I saw the little red MG at the bottom of the driveway. By the time he was at the door, I'd tried three or four hiding places. But no matter, Iris cried with glee when she heard his voice and ran to Papa. How could she know? Why should she know? He made a point of being nice and promised that he'd leave me be if I come back to Eugene, bring Iris back so he could be her dad. He is seeing a counselor. He will behave.

I haven't forgotten his swinging arms, his anger, and the sting of his slaps. But lying in my loft at night watching the stars through the skylight, I try to make sense of the failure of our relationship. Iris will start school in a couple years. I could still get my teaching license, start my own school, or find work anyplace we live.

If I stay here in this backwoods place, Iris won't have any opportunities but to live among the rednecks, the meth heads. In the city, we'll both have options. I can't support her for the rest of our days making cowboy shirts on a treadle sewing machine. I can't make her spend her childhood in 'squalor' as my mother so nicely put it. My car is about to give out. Stan says he has a lead on a Volkswagen bug I could pick up for less than two-hundred dollars. I give in. I give up. I give over to the inevitable like the downward course of flowing water.

Back in Eugene, he and I slip back into a routine—share Iris every other weekend like civilized people. He has a new girlfriend, and I'm off the hook unless he goes off the deep end and breaks into my house, scaring off any male visitors, day or night, which he has already done. I put up with it, again and again.

I hear the door handle. I feel my heart beating in my chest. I see his silhouette through the bedroom door and my heart is in my mouth. It reminds me of my childhood as a bed wetter—Dad coming into my room in the dark of night, the dread of being discovered in the puddle that has turned from warm and comforting to cold and ominous.

I drive my new blue bug back and forth to classes, back and forth to our new home in one of the old house trucks sitting empty in the backyard of one of our Bus Farm friends who bought a proper house and parked the bus out back—perfect for Iris and me until I find a teaching job. It's rough. But I feel tough and determined. I study at night by kerosene lamplight, sometimes in the freezing cold in the middle of winter.

One night I turn the damper down on the stove so it will keep the bus warm all night while we sleep. I awake coughing on thick smoke. The stove is leaking. I grab Iris and a blanket and with the door and windows open, we huddle on the back steps in below freezing temperatures until the place airs out.

The car barely runs—breaks down. I give in and ask Stan for help. The next day, while Iris is in day care, he follows me to the auto shop where he works. It's one of those rare sunny and warm autumn afternoons. We're traveling about 20 miles an hour down a side street in Eugene approaching a busy intersection. I check the rearview mirror. He's still behind me. The light turns red, and I press the brake pedal, but nothing happens—like a knife slicing whipped cream. I try again. Nothing. I'm heading toward the intersection and the red light; not a moment to think. The rusted-out Volkswagen bug putters and blows smoke. I throw open the door, tumble over the curb, tucking and rolling across a grass lawn as my car careens through the intersection and crashes into a garden of rocks and boulders in front of the house on the far side of the other street.

I've seen it in movies. James Bond leaps, tucks, rolls, and disappears. His Porche tumbles off a cliff—nothing left behind but a jacket or shirt dangling from a tree limb. I come to rest in the grass.

The dust settles, and I can barely muster the nerve to look. I've just flung myself from a moving car. What damage have I caused? Have I killed someone? I hear nothing but the sound of traffic on 18th Avenue but imagine terrible scenarios. Stan lurches toward me across someone's lawn, eyes afire and face twisted with a terrifying lack of sympathy. I venture a look at my car that has careened across the intersection, smoking and coughing where it's come to rest on a pile of rocks in someone's garden. I squint, but am afraid; have I killed someone?

My hands are bleeding and my entire body hurts. Stan doesn't take his eyes off me as I rub my knee, lick my palm, and listen to the man I once loved ranting and raving. He doesn't ask me why I leapt from the car, or if I'm OK.

He finally has the proof he needs—I am crazy. There are witnesses—undeniable corroboration. Have I not, for no apparent reason, jumped from a moving automobile? How is he to trust me with a four-year-old child?

Let's review: I applied the brake, the light turned red, nothing transpired. No drag, no stop. Peddle to the metal, a red light. So, like any quick-thinking agent, or responsible mother trying to stay alive, I jumped—applied my best tumbling maneuvers learned in high school—head of that class for sure.

I always laugh 'till I cry when I tell this story; sometimes until I can no longer breathe. It was 40-some years ago I leapt from that car, and I've carried on making live-or-die decisions—hasty bets on the workings of a complex and mysterious world. There are times I tucked when I should have rolled or rolled when I should have stayed put.

When we're in our thirties, we trust that there are countless chances and choices ahead. The awareness that we're living at light speed doesn't sink in until we're collecting Social Security. All those years ago, as I sat there in the grass watching Stan stride toward me, I was witnessing—not for the first or last time—the end of a life. I had failed, in his opinion, to tame and domesticate.

I've learned to go with the flow and if that means jumping, I jump. Panic never felt like a useful emotion. Life is complex and often thorny. Sometimes we spend too much time and energy trying to figure it out. I'm no Simone de Beauvoir.

It wasn't long after that incident I was hanging out with my girlfriends one night drinking beer and "yacking ninety." We decided it would be a good idea to make a break from the past, a break from the father of our children who physically or emotionally beat the crap out of us. It must have been a few weeks later in the middle of the night as I was sitting in front of a blaze in the fireplace that someone called my name, "Camille!"

"What?" I replied. From that day forward I've been Camille. I didn't leave Nancy in the dust; I will always love her. But changing my name from Nancy to Camille felt like a fresh start. From now on I would make better decisions. Maybe Camille, I thought, would be the adult version of Nancy.

It turns out, when I leapt from that car, tucked and rolled across a sidewalk and a front lawn, there was damage. My

Ready to party at the fair.

neck hurt. Though I was lucky to have not broken any bones, I ached all over and finally made an appointment to see my friend, Janie, a massage and Reiki therapist.

Lying on her massage table, Janie and I chat about this and that. I tell her Iris and I are living in the bottom floor of a friend's house up on the Point—a walk-in basement apartment with a great view, but I'm sleeping on a mattress on the floor.

Avner the Eccentric. Photo by Shandra Goodpasture Officer

"That can't be helping your neck," she says.

"I know. I know."

"You know our friend, Jim, right?" she says.

"Sure. I think he lives down near the bottom of our hill, by the university."

"Yep, with Ben and Jim's sister, Judy. And you know what? I bet you anything if you offered to cook him dinner, he'd be more than willing to make you a bed frame, get you up off that cold floor."

"Huh. I might do that. Just dinner?"

"Sure. Jim's always up for a good meal. I'll give you his phone number."

There's a pile of used lumber out back next to the garage—two-by-four scraps, unused sheets of plywood. I point Jim in that direction and go back to the kitchen to work on the casserole—mostly leftovers and tomato sauce. I hear Jim and Iris bantering back and forth.

After dinner he's down on the floor accommodating her requests for pony rides. I'm surprised when she goes to bed

Me and Jim.

willingly, listens to his stories about Mexico and Peru and the wide-eyed children he met there last year.

He and I talk late into the night about the Iranian hostage debacle, about Roe vs. Wade and the Supreme Court, the death of John Lennon, about Ronald Reagan and why it is we've wound up with a Hollywood insider as president. I always had the impression Jim was sort of a goofy guy, good looking and all, but goofy. Instead, I discover an intelligence—I see his tall thin frame take on the stance of thoughtful acumen as we stand by the wall of windows and look out over city lights below that blink beneath a blanket of stars.

At the door, he asks if I'd like to go out sometime. Sure, I say, and he calls about a week later. We plan a day at the coast. I don't remember the hour-long ride, due west about 50 miles, but I remember sitting on the beach until the sun set and into the night, talking and touching and falling in love.

And like soft butter on a hot bun, he melts into my life. And though Iris balks at his attempts to play Dad—You're not my father!— he participates in parent meetings at school, entertains her friends with his antics, and I soon forget my life as a single mom, forget the feelings of loneliness I've felt since I was four years old. We find a vintage two-story house near Iris's grade school. There's a garden in the walled-in backyard covered in wisteria; we each have a room upstairs overlooking a thick planting of trees, flowers, and vegetables. There are days we lie together on his bed and drift, listen to the birds, soak in our happiness.

It's nice to have an extra set of arms and legs to help me in the spring with the History Booth at the Oregon Country Fair (*nee* the Renaissance Faire). I launched the booth last year. I hang framed pictures taken over the years by local photographer, Shandra Goodpasture Officer, install artifacts and memorabilia. People keep asking where they might get their own T-shirt—the kind the staff wears with the Fair logo on the front. So I convince the board of directors to let me produce and sell commemorative T-shirts. The first T-shirt year, fans line up to get a shirt—four-deep wide rows looping out into the dusty path.

Jim and I sleep in our loft over the booth; we let our friends party there during the day. At night we lie on our bed and holler back and forth across the wide bend in the dirt path to the guys who stay up all night at Fair Central; listen to the static of their walkie-talkies, and by the middle of the night we manage to fall asleep despite the ruckus. I will be up at the crack of dawn to haul T-shirts, organize crew, hang pictures, and decorate the booth. Gates will open at 11:00 a.m.

The Country Fair is something we look forward to every year. Even though I'm busy with my teaching career, Fair business takes up lots of space and energy in our household—phone ringing, committees meeting, posters and signs under construction in the living room.

Our lives are full in the way thirty-something and forty-something peoples are. We have children and they have friends. We have a family of friends closer than any blood tribe. We have energy to spare. We party; ideas turn into projects—even a publishing company at one point. Our house is always hopping. We don't understand this will end one day—a benchmark that takes empty nesters by surprise.

The day of our wedding is one Saturday at the Oregon Country Fair, the second weekend in July. We're hanging out in our shady loft, taking a break from hours of hauling shirts and posters from Main Camp to the History Booth, managing crew, counting money, and answering questions until I'm ready to drop. We are lying on our backs watching leaves in the ancient oak tree above our loft flutter in the breeze. The wash of fresh air is a relief from the determined July heat. One of us says, "Let's get married." One of us says, "Let's ask Reverend Chumleigh."

Like pulling a curtain open and entering a hollow without a note of hesitation, we're off and hunting down the irreverent New Age Vaudevillian—henchman for the Miraculous Church of the Incandescent Resurrection.

The Reverend is eating a Rita's burrito out behind the Main Stage. We approach. We pose our brainchild—then wait and watch as his eyes dart from treetop to treetop. He looks at us. "I'll do it . . . You'll be my act tonight . . . Midnight Show. Perfect." The momentum for an historical event is set in

Reverend Chumleigh officiating our wedding from the tightrope.

motion. " . . . didn't know what I was going to do." He wipes his goatee free of sprouts and beans and walks off.

We spend the rest of the day spreading the word, registering for wedding gifts at craft booths and having our fingers measured for wedding rings at the silversmiths. My pal Sheila will be my maid of honor. She will dress me later. I have work to do.

People come by bringing gifts and enough bottles of champagne to prime the party later, after closing time, after The Sweep. My one-time love, Lightning, will give me away. Jim's friend Maida will be his Best Person.

Daylight fades and energy for the event flourishes like a bonfire in the wind. There has never been a wedding at the Country Fair. Someone from Entertainment Crew stops by the History Booth to tell us to come down the back road, the service road, later that night—around twelve thirty. "No flashlights, no lanterns. We don't want anyone to see you or distract from the show."

By the time the Midnight Show finally gets off the ground, there will be hundreds of staff people spread out on blankets covering the field around Main Stage—lemmings in search of sea water. The Midnight Show is what every Country Fair staffer waits for—all year long, all day long on Saturday of the Fair. For some, it's what they come for—the most outrageous new age vaudevillian show in all the land—Mud Bay Jugglers, Karamazov Brothers, Artis the Spoonman, Reverend Chumleigh, Bubble Man; sword swallowers, fire-eaters. It's R-rated, unlike the daytime G-rated shows.

A womb of darkness engulfs the backwoods. A gang of my friends and Jim's friends are congregated at the head of Moz Road, just off Chickadee Lane. They're whispering, but I'm speechless, surrendering like a child to the control of these people who I've come to trust over the years—Lightning and Brian, Sheila, Maida—shadows who take hold of me and guide me along the rutted dirt road. I'm too exhausted and too stunned at what is happening to function on my own. Tripping on tree roots and stumbling over stones and who knows what, I let them pull me and hold me upright like a game of trust. I wish Iris were here, but she's at Camp Winnarainbow.

People shush each other as the road narrows to a path, and the sound of juggling clubs and waves of laughter gets louder and louder until we're at the gates of Back Stage Security where people block the entrance.

"Let them in. It's Camille and Jim."

"Shhhh . . ."

"Chumleigh . . ."

"Shhush . . ."

The small clearing behind the stage is surrounded by ancient oak trees. Security staff nod and smile. Chumleigh turns and grins. He's standing at the stairway leading to the back of the stage. He's wearing a leopard skin leotard. Barefoot. He looks serious—giving instructions to three large guys, swinging his arms, pointing in our direction. He looks around. He motions for us to come over.

"We'll play this by ear. I need everyone's name who's going to be onstage." He doesn't write anything down.

The stage lights are bright, and I'm blinded. I hear the throngs out there, but I see only a veil of darkness. Cheers rise into the night and the chill air. Chumleigh says something about the solemnity of the occasion. "No accounting for taste, folks!" The crowd roars, and he bounds into a soliloquy about the tightrope of marriage and asks the assembly on stage-left to hold one end of an actual tightrope, the other end is tied to a tree at stage right.

He considers this ragtag crew holding the rope, puts his hand to his heart. "I trust you," he says. The crowd howls.

Lights flicker throughout a sea of people.

"Who gives this woman in holy matrimony?"

"I do," says Lightning.

"Her Ex!" says the Reverend, inching his way toward his makeshift tightrope. "Only in Eugene!" Another explosion swells from the dark.

I watch Chumleigh feign to test the rope. It's his show. A unified gasp rises and falls. It occurs to me that we've saved a lot of money on invitations. I'm holding a glowing battery-run rose someone has put into my hands; it glitters—I clutch it to my chest.

"A glowing rose!" the Reverend says. "Take the lady's hand and give her your promise."

Jim's words come fast. "I love you."

I've but one thing to say in return. "I love you too."

A unanimous "Awwwwww" wafts over the meadow.

Chumleigh's on the rope in his leopard skin leotard, arms outstretched, and the people holding the taught twine strain with his weight as he shouts above our heads, "By the power invested in me by the Church of the Incandescent Resurrection, I pronounce you Permanent Partners 'till the cows come home!"

The crowd thunders. Bubble Man, who's been waiting behind us, engulfs Jim and me in a giant bubble that somehow stays intact long enough to present the intended effect. Undulating cheers, and the Country Fair band plays "Picnic time for teddy bears, the little teddy bears are having a wonderful time today . . . today's the day the teddy bears are having their picnic!"

Jim takes me, wraps his arms around me and we kiss. I feel his warmth—his arms are shaking. There's applause and the band marches away through the sea of Fair Family folks in a blur—people sitting and lying on blankets and grass and even beyond the edge of the expanse of the Main Stage meadow. They've waited for this moment until two in the morning.

8

I'm up at my friend Nicki's one afternoon. Nicki and her husband, Rock Scully, managed the Grateful Dead road show for years. You never know who you might run into at her garden retreat on the top of the hill in South Eugene where she is building a shaman business—a hands-on healing empire. It doesn't hurt business that she is still involved with the Dead. She provides her own form of participatory stage show as part of Shamanic Journeys—vision quests, guided meditation journeys, and personal totem animals. There is a steady stream of friends, clients, and Deadheads.

Nicki and I study the healing art of Huna together under Nadia Eagles, a beautiful dark-haired woman with other-worldly qualities. We meet in her living room every week—a circle of students. She teaches us to move energy, to feel disease inside someone's body, to throw it away and replace it with positive light. Huna is an ancient healing practice that originated in Africa, she says, and made its way, at some point long ago, to the Hawaiian Islands. I take notes. Sometimes I fall asleep, but Nadia says I'll get it whether I am awake or asleep; I am taking it all in. With her guidance, we take journeys to places in our subconscious.

I am in the woods, following a narrow path upwards. The trail is overgrown with ferns and moss-covered branches, ancient lichen rubbing against my face as I walk. I am searching for a secret entrance to a cave in the side of the mountain. I find it where she said it would be. Barely winded from the arduous climb, I make cautious steps into an ancient chamber. I sit down on a rock covered with moss. I feel as though I've been here before. Great Aunt Marion is sitting on another stone bench, facing me. She beckons me, her arms outstretched. As though expecting her, I go to her and sit close to my beloved aunt, like all those nights so long ago by the fire in her living room, absorbing the warmth of her love. I look up, and there on another bench is my grandmother, young and beautiful, yet recognizable. A window, a sort of portal, at the far end of the chamber lets in shards of light—soft starlight. Grandma bids me to look out over the abyss into infinity. She motions for me to move closer to the opening. Though it had been daylight when I entered, a night sky gleams through the portal. Stars flicker and glow as I gaze out over the void of eternity. I am home. I am here.

The afternoon I meet Hagen up at Nicki's, she and I are exploring things we could do with her new computer. During the mid-1980s, personal computers are new. I race downstairs to exclaim about something called a database.

She is out on the deck with a gray-haired man. He has an open and friendly face, a twinkle in his eye. Nicki introduces me to Mike Hagen. I go over to take his hand and he looks up at me, holds onto my hand and says he's looking for someone to type a manuscript for him. "Do you type for money?" he asks.

His hand is warm. "Only for love," I reply.

Late afternoon the next day the phone rings. "We met yesterday," Hagen's voice teases. He repeats his name and I remember where I've heard it years ago when I read the

Electric Kool-Aid Acid Test on the Greyhound bus on the way to
Denver, running away from Tom.

"Look, I've got this cowboy story and I need help with the
typing."

"I'm really more into editing," I say. "But I suppose I could
do both."

"Hot dog. That would really be great. I'll pay you."

"Well, whatever."

"How about lunch tomorrow?"

He promises to pick me up around noon. I can tell he's the
kind of guy who could and would do something crazy. "Think
of a good place," he says. I think of San Francisco, Paris, or
maybe the Country Inn, 50 miles upriver.

By 12:30 the next day we're at the 6th Street Bar and Grill
in downtown Eugene drinking Bloody Marys. He drinks two
before I decide what to order for lunch which turns into
more cocktails, and Mike downs two or three for every one
of mine. The room spins and through a river of enthusiastic
conversation he tells me about his schemes—a complicated
plan to write an exposé about Oliver North, to make a video
of his trial which will implicate scoundrels like Ronald Reagan
and John Poindexter. He has the connections. He can't wait
for me to meet Lynn, his hotshot writer friend who is taking
Kesey's novel-writing class. The three of us could collaborate,
go to the East Coast—hire a producer. He has experience with
a camera—he filmed the Prankster's heyday.

We drink more Bloody Marys. Then we drive fast along
Route 58 to his place in Pleasant Hill—a pint-size trailer house
behind a barn down a country road. Hagen pours more booze,
and we talk and laugh at his kitchen table, never running out of
banter or zeal for a newfound friendship.

I want to go home, but I'm having too much fun. Much later, way later, I limp into my house in the middle of the night. Jim will be mad, possibly hurt. I crawl into bed, slip under the covers and cozy up to my husband. "That took a while," he says.

"I'm sorry. We were having a good time, and . . ."

"Don't worry. He was my hero back in the day." He rolls over and takes me in his arms.

We never did expose Oliver North, Ronald Reagan, or John Poindexter, but we did have a hand in shutting down a nuclear power plant. That is all I can say about that.

I met Mountain Girl (MG) on an early spring afternoon. My friend Hal said he wanted me to meet a friend. "She just moved back from the Bay Area." He believes we'll hit it off. "Let's think of something special to do together," he says.

A few days later, my brother Peter, who lives about 40 miles south in a small logging and mill town off Highway 34, calls to say that they're having a pool tournament at the Chug-a-Lug. I should get some friends together and come down, join the fun. Virgil is going to DJ, and his wife, Gracie, the bartender, will be serving two 'fers—there will be food and fun and plenty of local color.

I convince Hal, and he persuades MG, that this will be a blast. So it happened that we drove to Pleasant Hill that day to retrieve a six-foot powerhouse and head down the freeway sipping from a canning jar of homemade blackberry wine she brought along.

And we do hit it off. Our feet resting on the dashboard, we drink electric blackberry wine, hoot and chortle, and by the

time Hal eases the old Suburban into the last parking spot at
the Chug, most of the contents of that jar has been consumed.
The world sparkles. I feel woozy but remember to tell Hal, as
we're sliding out of the truck, about to enter the front door,
that I've signed him up for the pool tournament. "No big
deal," I say, a vain effort to quell the panic in his eyes. "You can
whoop their sorry asses."

The place is hopping and stomping and there are bikers
toting pool sticks in every corner of this country tavern. MG
and I head for an opening at the far corner of the bar, and she
takes refuge on a comfortable-looking barstool at the end of
the long wooden slab, belches, and looks around.

"Oh, I don't know if I would sit there," someone says. MG
pulls out her Swiss Army knife, cleans her nails, and calls to
Crazy for a pitcher of beer.

"Her name is Gracie," I whisper loudly over the din, but
MG doesn't seem to hear, and neither does Gracie who draws
a pint from the red tap.

"That's Big D's stool," my brother comes up behind us
hoping to save our skins, hoping to keep the peace. The thing
is, according to bar lore, Big D is a biker with an injured
leg from the war, and this barstool was made just for him.
"He gets out of sorts if anyone trespasses." MG clearly isn't
concerned about Big D, or that she's sitting in his seat.

Gracie slides the beer down the shiny wooden bar. "I don't
give a hoot if I never see that goddamned Jesus-freakin' liberal
in here again!"

MG and I are two hilarious hyenas, consuming who knows
how many pints of brew. In comes Big D. He looks MG up
and down and up close, starts to speak, and then MG smiles
and asks what he'll be drinking. The bar crowd pauses, as if

a movie reel has broken, but it's already evident that Big D is smitten with this Mountain Girl sittin' on his seat. She can sit there as long as she wants.

Virgil's running a turntable and talking to the crowd on a mic over in the corner. He plays "Leader of the Pack," and when the song is done, he reminds the bunch about tomorrow's bass derby. Another biker sidles up next to me and says, "Throw that damn bait back in with the rest of the pickled peckers at the Cold Point Market, would you?"

Someone over by the pool table shouts, "Where's my cue?

Another biker says, "Let's get on with the pool tournament." And the action starts up again.

Virgil answers a question from the pack. "Will, he's on the wagon. And by the way, it's your shot Vanessa."

Gracie turns on the TV over the bar. It's Oral Roberts and he's asking us to open our hearts and our wallets. Gracie flicks it off again. Virgil smiles at her and asks who put the last nine holes in Mussolini's body.

Hours later, after MG has won the affection of every logger and biker in the bar, after Hal manages to save face and hit a few balls into the side pockets; long after the evening is over, the Suburban deposits us at my house. I have no way to explain how we made it home, but we partied on for the rest of the night. We wrote a play for our future entertainment and possible fame, *The Tale of MG, the Bartender Named Crazy, and the Bar Stool Belonging to Big D.*

Around four in the morning, Jim came downstairs, sleepy-eyed but smiling. He made a pot of coffee, and the four of us played Scrabble until the sun came up, something we would do frequently after that night.

Not long ago I came across the original manuscript of the play, scribbled on and dribbled on, but memorable enough to be recognizable at once. There, for a moment, I was back in the company of a gang who thought there was nothing more side-splitting than whiling away an afternoon squishing Fruit Loops through the cracks on the front porch of Hal's family cabin at Fish Lake or trawling for fish in the twilight out on the lake—celebrating another Solstice with a fresh bottle of homemade blackberry wine. Those were the days.

A close group formed the way you do in your 30s and 40s. We did everything together. When our friend Sidney died of a brain tumor leaving behind three bewildered children, a group of us made her coffin.

She would be buried at the top of Cougar Mountain, a communal property owned by several in our gang not far from the original Bus Farm. A couple weeks before she died and we were all up there, though she could no longer speak, she made it clear to a couple of us that she wanted to go up the hill where she would be buried. We pushed her in the wheelchair up a rutted muddy road, stopping to look at mushrooms and other wildlife along the steep climb. It was a stretch, we huffed and pushed and somehow made it over rocks and ruts to the sunny meadow at the top of the mountain.

After she died, her husband, Jerry, a county commissioner, and a few other close friends who had been tree planters, crafted a beautiful wooden coffin made of yew wood and delivered it to my house. The coffin had been Noah's idea, one of the kids in our clan. A group of us women gathered with carefully selected swatches of our personal stashes of fabrics, laces, and other collectables we chose to wrap our sister in for her journey. We got to work lining the handsome coffin, agates and other gems inlaid on the lid. "Let's use this blue satin for the inside of the lid." Tangerine held up the fabric for better judgment.

"We could make white puffy clouds," I said. Everyone agreed on both counts. Each swatch of velvet or Lebanese quilting and antique silk was glued or stitched or worked carefully into a soothing landscape to embrace our dear sister.

"She'll forever have blue skies," Erica spoke softly as we finished.

"Ain't it the truth."

"I'd do this for you, too," I said to no one in particular as I leaned my chin on the edge of the yew wood coffin.

"Me too," everyone added one at a time while we stared at the empty space inside the box.

Jim died a few years later, and that was the second time he left me in one year. It was the mid-1990s. Please don't go, I pleaded when he left for Hawaii. But the day he died, I would not ask him to stay—surely he wanted to this time. None of the small stuff we had come to bicker over in the days before he went away mattered anymore.

The day he left for Hawaii he packed all his things in boxes. Occasionally I stumble upon a box of his in the garage, or during a move. I tighten up the bags, rearrange the paraphernalia, the pictures, journals, a box of nails, small mementos. Maybe if I could have kept his boxes intact . . . I find ways to blame myself or make sense out of what happened. I still wonder whatever happened to his tool belt. Jim was tall and skinny and when he wore it, weighted down with hammer, nails, and tape measure, it hung low on his hips—as though about to fall, like low-slung jeans in a fashion ad. This is how I remember him—happy and smiling at me, tool belt hanging low, the sun shining. I understand now that he was pulled to the tropics because he didn't feel good. Like a sick dog, he wanted to hide, to be warm.

Almost one year to the day after he left us to live the life of an itinerant writer on the beaches of Maui, he was diagnosed with testicular cancer. Turns out he had been ignoring a lump and other discomforts until he couldn't disregard them anymore. He made his first doctor visit on a sunny sultry day, a day like any other in his new world. He told me later that on his way home, that time, he saw the colors and smelled the aroma of the abundant Hawaiian flowers in a way he had never before—the way people do when they come face-to-face with mortality. Like something that's been hiding in the bushes, it popped out and hollered "boo!"

When he got so sick, he couldn't live on his own anymore, he came back, stayed with friends while he struggled through the last part of the awful sickness. Doctors tried removing part of his stomach and a kidney, but the disease persisted. He'd had so many rounds of chemo there was nothing left of him but skin on bone.

For two months, maybe longer, he spent his days surrounded by friends and family, lying on the hospital bed David and Nancy set up for him in a spare room. The view out the bedroom window was alive with walnut trees drooping with fruit and shaking with the antics of squirrels. Some mornings, steam rose from the hot tub outside the French doors on the deck, mixing with the chill air just after sunrise. He and I would lie together on the bed, my arm around his frail middle. Love prevails. Though his body shouted the inevitable, we didn't talk about the dying; we didn't talk about what was really on our minds. I know now that we were both still a little angry about the failure of our marriage, what we perceived as the other's fault, or the disappointment of our separation. Mostly we were sorry and sad.

One afternoon I helped him into the large wooden vat of hot water and chlorine out on the deck. The sight of his skeleton brought tears to my eyes, reminded me of my possible guilt in the matter. I wasn't sure what I was guilty of exactly, but certain of my culpability.

This sense of guilt has been part of me as far back as I can remember, and a nagging feeling of the unpredictable nature of love, of life. As Leary once told me, we need each other to maneuver the chaos of life, but ultimately, we do it alone.

I had guilt dreams as a child. I remember one as though I slept through it last night instead of sixty-some years ago. I woke in the middle of the night, six years old and alone in my shadowy room, sweating and shaking. It had been a bad day, and now a bad night. In my dream—my nightmare—my younger sister, Mary, and I were clutching and yanking on my Tiny Tears doll. She had been wanting, demanding, that doll ever since I opened it on Christmas morning. Hers was different, had hair and mine did not. She liked mine better. This Tiny Tears was the only doll I ever enjoyed, as far as dolls go. I didn't want to share. My parents said that nice little girls share. That night, when Dad tucked me in, he added that nice girls don't trespass and steal flowers from the neighbors. I am not a nice girl.

I slept fitfully in a puddle of pee. My dream raged on, Mary and I were tugging, back and forth, each clutching one of the

Me and Mary.

doll's arms, pulling and crying. One of the doll's arms popped out into my hands. I fell backwards onto the floor clutching my two-year-old sister's bloody arm, my own sister's arm. There in the bed, cold, alone; afraid to move, afraid to breathe, I felt my body turn to stone.

I must have lay there wide-eyed most of the night. As morning neared, the sound of crickets beat a high-pitched rhythm down on the lawn, a hollow echo in my empty world. I was certain my sister was dead, had bled to death in the crib in the next room, and it was all my fault.

The day Jim died we had never talked about this permanent going away. I sat as still as I could on the side of his tall bed, my feet groping for a place to rest on the side railings. His breath came irregularly in rasping gasps. Someone approached and administered another eyedropper of morphine. People moved about the house, and a constant murmur of voices wafted from the living room. His buddies, his baseball teammates, kept vigil on the couch in the corner of the bedroom.

Nicki and I crafted a guided meditation the night before to give to Jim at the time of his death—the journey for Jim's dying—wrote it down on paper so I would remember the details when things got tough. We didn't want to leave him floundering as he tried to find his way to the other side.

"Jim," I whisper softly as I lean over him on the bed. "Are you ready to take a journey?"

"Yes." This is the first time he has acknowledged he is not going to make it. I take hold of his hand, hold it gently. It feels like paper, soft pliable paper.

"Try to let go," I say quietly so the others won't hear. My voice is shaking. His eyes are closed, but I see them flutter. I remember the time we hiked to the top of the mountain in Klamath County down in Southern Oregon to interview the tree sitter who'd been up there for most of the summer—the last part of the trek, straight up. I was proud that I didn't have to stop too often for a breath, but it was a haul anyway. Jim was lean and muscular and could have run all the way up that slope, but he was patient and stopped when I needed to stop.

I continue. "You are weightless as air. Jim, feel yourself rise like smoke from a campfire. Can you let yourself go?" In my mind, I see water seeping through rocks as the ocean tide goes out. It's dark in my vision, midnight.

He stirs. Sunlight brightens the room, accenting its silence. I have left my own body and am watching this drama unfold from a new perspective. I can't believe it's happening. But I go on. "Like the speed of light, you fly and soar on the wings of Hathor."

His eyelids pulse again, only slightly this time. I am with him, and we soar above the clouds. I see water below, soft white clouds, a distant landscape, and I wonder how far I'll go. Then I hang back inside my own body.

"Jim? Cling gently. Hathor holds you firmly on the great expanse of his large outstretched and glistening wings. They are raven black. Now the two of you fly beneath the sun and above the endless waters of all that you have been, in this life here, and all that you will be for all time." The room is quiet as death. Someone coughs. Someone takes in a mouthful of air.

I watch with dread and anticipation as his chest moves up and down, imperceptibly. I think about his life and about our life together. He was good with a hammer and saw. He built beautiful cabinets, could fix anything. He was good with paper and pen. He wrote pieces about the environment for magazines and newspapers, about the subject of how corporate America wreaks havoc on forests and streams. He had a regular column in the *High Country News*. He wrote travel pieces, sometimes published in airline magazines or the San Jose *Mercury News*. This gave him a break to get out and move around the world. Sometimes I went with him, but mostly he traveled alone. He liked solitude when he worked, and he liked lots of friends around when he played. Sometimes we took Iris and her friend Trixie to interesting places up and down the west coast.

He played baseball; he swam in the frigid Oregon rivers. He once hiked the mountains of Peru. He took startling pictures of people he loved and people he met in small villages in foreign places.

We hang there for a second, for an eternity. I feel like a small child who has scared herself in the dark. Without saying anything else, I leave the room, go to the kitchen, and wait for him to die. There is a quiet corner at a small table next to a window. I sit and gaze at the large backyard. It hasn't been mowed in some time. The only sound I hear is the thumping of my heart, its rapid beat echoing inside my ears.

I gaze at the squirrels running and jumping from tree to tree. A small raincloud overtakes the faint glow of the low-slung harvest sun. Someone cries out from the bedroom. Without moving from the chair, without moving my gaze from the trees, I begin to rearrange my world, the whole world. There's a steady current of teardrops on the table where I lean over and wrap my arms around my stomach. Despite all the build up to this dying, I don't know how I'm supposed to feel or what will come next. I am certain of my categorical guilt.

It's his time to go.

Later, the day Jim died, I find myself standing still on a farm road behind a worn-out orchard, listening to the rustling of a grassy field. It is a soft breeze, and the field is shades of green and brown against a backdrop of scrub oak trees. Wispy clouds swirl past as I wonder where Jim has gone, where we all go one day. A bee, or some kind of bug, buzzes next to my ear and lands on a bush by the side of the road—unconcerned about anything but that bush. It pays me no heed. Maybe it senses my turmoil and moves on, away from this odd disturbance.

That night, I dream of my father. He is angry with me. He doesn't love me anymore. My mother had told him of things I have done, how I have made her miserable. I reach for him, but he turns away. I watch his back as he disappears down Parsons Drive. I hop on my bike, the blue and red bike on which he taught me to ride down the sidewalk that had once been a farm road through my great grandfather's place. I peddle like crazy trying to catch up, but no matter how hard, how desperately I pursue, he is no longer reachable. He is gone.

9

A girl I hardly know corners me in the hallway of the high school. "Mike LoBello wants to go out with you." My cheeks burn while a crowd of girls press in close to hear my answer. I have never considered such a thing happening to me. Will he call; will he ask me to the Saturday night dance? Should I approach him? I have no idea what to do. I wait, enlist the help of my best friend, Kathie, who joins me in an ongoing conversation—on the phone, lying on my bedroom floor, walking home after school—Mike LoBello, the exclusive topic of discussion.

One afternoon while we sit talking about certain details discovered about his life—12 brothers and sisters, an absent father, a tumbled-down house by the lake—I spot him through my bedroom window walking with a gang of boys heading into the driveway of the house down the dirt road beside our house where a boy named Goose lives.

Kathie and I take guard at the window after school and on the weekends, crouching and peering cautiously above the windowsill. When he appears, we throw ourselves onto the floor. Later, I lie in bed next to this window and replay each sighting. Why have I never seen him at Goose's house before?

He and I begin running into each other uptown, in the hall between classes, on the front steps of the school, at the soda fountain. I feel the inevitable I cannot name. Soon, we are always together. We hold hands. I am his girl.

At the end of my junior year, it is made clear by the music teacher I am going to star in the all-school play next year. Three of my paintings are hanging in a gallery in downtown Syracuse. It's a promising young artist's exhibition at the art museum. But on the first day of my senior year, instead of Senior Homeroom, I'm sitting in a small, musty office with

Me at nine months taking my first steps in front of the elm tree swing.

my parents in Buffalo, miles away from the small town, the school, and Mike. I fix my eyes on a pair of red rubber boots in the corner. The room is thick with an uncomfortable silence except for the change jingling in my father's pockets. I wonder what Mike is doing. Why didn't he call me back?

The door opens and I jump—a social worker enters with a trickle of fresh air and closes it with a sharp click. My father extends his hand and his most polite manner. My mother says nothing, and I keep staring at the boot. My throat hurts. My ears ring, drowning out the conversation—drowning out what is being said about my impending stay at The Home. I am in trouble. Mike needled me for sex for years, but my response was always something like, "God wouldn't like it." He was an altar boy, didn't he understand?

One night he said, "Don't you know that everyone does it? Bob and Bonnie, Doug and Sue, you name it, they all do it." I was shocked. These were my friends. Why hadn't they told me? For weeks and months, he pushed the matter, but I was afraid. Finally, I gave in. I didn't want to lose him, unaware that that he was hound-dogging around behind my back anyway—all along.

After my parents leave, I stand in the hallway with the social worker. It's quiet. I can hear the elevator creaking down the shaft. The door slides open,

I decide to go for it.

Me, Mary, and brother Bob.

and she holds it in place, waiting for me to pick up my suitcase and do what is expected of a girl in my position. Everything echoes in this place.

Alone in the dark little room overlooking a park, I look around and take in the single bed with the metal frame, stained bedspread, and the linoleum floor. The curtains are faded gray. They may have once had flowers, but just dingy now. I walk over to the window and peer through an opening in the flimsy fabric. Down in the garden there are rows of neatly pruned rose bushes—spent lilacs hang like sad dogs, and withered iris blooms droop

Me and Mary at the swing.

over a small duck pond. The cracked and crumbling cement edges are covered with moss. A young woman pushes a baby carriage along the sidewalk.

Months later, I gave birth to a girl in a lonely room in a strange hospital. A different social worker stood by my bed as I held the baby I had named Angela. I wanted her to have an angel to look after her. The social worker tapped her feet, waiting for me to sign the papers, waiting to take the tiny baby away.

I didn't see Mike again for a long time, and perhaps Kathie was too busy to hang out anymore. I never saw Angela again, no matter how hard I tried to find her.

I've heard the phrase 'sea change' used to describe a transformation in one's life that's significant, yet unforeseen. It happens slowly, over time. Imperceptibly. The shift is a result of a series of events, or one event that we have no control over—no way of knowing how forever changed our lives will be once it has occurred. The expression originates from Shakespeare's Tempest:

Full fathom five thy father lies;
Of his bones are coral made;
Those are pearls that were his eyes:
Nothing of him that doth fade
but doth suffer a sea-change
into something rich and strange.

One person can have as powerful a bearing on our life's course as the sea may wrought on what it captures in its potent wake. Someone passes through and without warning we are a different person, longing for what was lost, waiting for something we can't name.

I once asked my mother how we are to cope in a world that's falling apart—when there are senseless wars, massive harm done to the environment by corporate America, when the man we love turns into someone we don't know. She said you have to have faith. You have to be able to believe without any supporting evidence that things will be okay. She and I probably define faith differently, but sometimes I suppose we must suspend disbelief or go mad.

Over the years, I've remembered this rare and tender conversation and the wise and caring response to this big question. I believe she was right and envy those who find this faith she was talking about—the best I have been able to do is hope. On days when the world is dark and bleak, I hope to find love, hope that my ship will come in, and most importantly, hope that the grown-ups that steer this ship we call a global society will one day find the wisdom to work as partners, rather than adversaries, to rescue the sinking ship—that these so-called grown-ups will be consistently trustworthy instead of criminals.

At the very heart of my extended family life— grandparents, aunts, uncles, and cousins—stood a gigantic elm tree in the center of my grandparents' backyard. A magnificent swing, so high in the tree it had to be hung at the start of each summer by the Volunteer Fire Department. They would arrive unannounced and ease their giant bucket truck down the driveway by the side of the house and into the backyard. In no time at all, the giant machine hoisted the rope and its swing—the magical instrument of flight. Once in place, the swing consisted of a simple wooden seat suspended by a thick rope. It was solid. It was the swing of poetry and childhood memories.

On any Sunday afternoon, we would gather on cane-bottomed lawn furniture around the base of the tree with my grandmother and grandfather, Aunt Marion, Uncle David, Aunt Wilma, and my cousins, Barbara, David, and John Peter. Most of the family photographs of those days take place on or next to the swing. My first step is captured as I tentatively let go of the swing and take a footstep out into the back yard, the beyond.

My father and Uncle David push all us cousins as high as we can go. They grab hold of the bottom of the swing and then run underneath while pushing us up to the very leaves on the upper branches of the elm tree. We scream with glee and hold on for dear life. At the end of the day, my cousin Barbara and I cling to each other at the front door, not wanting to ever end the fun and each other's company.

In the late 60s, after most of us have grown up, gone away—forgotten about the swing—a blight of Dutch Elm disease sweeps the upper Midwest and New England. The leaves at the top of my grandfather's tree begin to turn yellow and curl. At some point, a tree surgeon concluded that the tree would have to come down. My grandfather refuses. The tree was not coming down. No sir. That tree is staying right where it is. My father and Uncle David talk on the phone several times. My father goes over to talk with his father, alone. The tree is not coming down. It becomes sicker, more yellow. I hear my parents talking one day about one good windstorm, about the tree landing right on my grandparents' bedrooms one night while they sleep. Sometimes stiff winds whip off Skaneateles Lake in the middle of the night, sometimes during the day in hurricane weather.

One day, David drives down from Rochester. He and my father go together to confront their father. This must have been a daunting deed, for my grandfather was not inclined with humor. He was inclined to be stubborn. He was inclined to love that tree and what it represented. But as fate would have it, the tree came down. I could not bear to look at the empty spot after that. My grandfather died within the year and my grandmother less than two years later.

Today, in my mind's eye, I can sit on that swing, I can smell the breeze off the lake, hear the chickens clucking behind Baylor's barn, see my grandmother shelling peas on the back porch, and my throat aches. It aches for what is lost, or what might have been if the wind had blown us all one way instead of the other.

PART 2

Life is remembered in a series of scenes, of episodes, people, places, and most significantly, in eras. There is the era of our childhood, our coming of age, young adulthood, a family, parenthood; perhaps the dissolution of a marriage, even the loss of a child, and then to the day when we say this getting old business is for the birds. Memories are skewed. Fact becomes irretrievably mixed with a sort of fiction that is our life story. The story changes over time—not on purpose, but our mind plays tricks. We try to make sense of the chaos, to find the balance between who we are, who we once hoped to be, and what has been lost in the fury of time. The true facts are only a framework.

There is a young woman, a college student. She is a bit of a loner who imagines herself to be otherwise. She remains alone at the college dorm at Christmas time when everyone else has gone home. The darkest days for her have lingered after the solstice. Her boyfriend is in the war zone in Vietnam, and her own family does not notice that she is missing; the boyfriend has not noticed that she no longer loves him. She thinks now that she never did. She spends her time alone working on a painting she is making on a large slab of wood. Days pass, and she nears death from pneumonia of the body and soul. One

133

night, her fever is so high she sleeps by an open window in minus zero temperatures. In the morning, she is covered with a fine layer of powdery snow. The fever is broken.

I remember this young woman as though she were someone else. I was someone else. I had a long row to hoe to get to this part of my life. Truth is, I still tend to isolate, or perhaps now that I'm older I tend to isolate again—like I did as a child and a young woman alone in the world for the first time.

We are forever leaving something or someone or some place behind. Every morning yesterday is past, in our wake, in our hearts. But a handful of days are remembered with clarity—a smell, a song, a broken heart. I once heard someone say that all love ends in tears. One way or another, I suppose it does.

As we age, and I'm talking about slipping quietly into our 70s and then burning up years like flame to tissue paper, the tide does not wait for us to be ready. It goes out imperceptibly; you don't see it happening. As I go about my day, I relive time, the events in my past as they march or twitter through my mind unannounced. Some are joyful, some are sad, but in the reliving they are neither. They are the contents of a life. I might be doing the dishes or taking a bath and then there I am, back there. Sometimes I hear the rustle of maple leaves, the sound of an ancient tree creaking, bending, and swaying in the wind.

These giant trees line the street that passes my grandparent's house. In the summertime, they rustle in the sun as I ride the red wagon down the hill, over the bump in the sidewalk where the roots of one of the trees has pushed it apart; I come to a stop in front of Bailor's house. I am safe, but my grandmother, who stands at the door, is not sure. The wind picks up and the giant maples rage in the wild breeze. She calls me in. Grandpa retrieves the wagon and takes it down to the barn.

Sometimes the sound of a flag flapping in the breeze takes me to the schoolyard at Cherry Road. Sometimes it is the scraping of forks on plates, a chair scratching across the wooden floor in the dining room; a jazz singer; chatter, angry chatter; someone crying.

There are affairs in the world around me now on which I ruminate. A mentally ill president has marketed his paranoid delusions to somewhere around 70 million people who follow his lead. Psychologists have described it as the Truman Show Syndrome, or the Truman Show Delusion—a person who believes they are the center of the universe—are being watched and persecuted. Their lives are wrapped up in make-believe. In today's world, people with these psychological tendencies can be swayed by misinformation dished up on social media, Fox news, and worse yet, the President of the United States.

I don't want to be remembered as a hippie. I'd rather go down as an aware and intelligent person who put her life on the superhighway to capitalistic success aside to fight in small ways for a better world. Aging doesn't make one irrelevant, it takes one to a place where you can look back and measure. What did I do? Did I make a difference? What do I have to share now?

I did go on to teach young people. It wasn't my passion—it was more of a moral obligation. I was an idealist who painted a picture of the world and how I would fit in; I muddled through the terrain of professionalism you might say. The realities of high school social studies teaching in those days—the 1970s

135

I still had a long way to peddle in life.

and 80s—required that you double as a football or basketball coach. I once offered to be the ball, and eventually wound up promoting educational technology to classroom teachers.

At the International Society for Technology in Education I helped form partnerships with emerging tech companies, went to conferences and meetings around the country. At one conference hosted by *Fortune Magazine* in Washington, DC, I sat next to then Governor Bill Clinton—alphabetical seating.

I was there in place of my boss who couldn't attend. I had the uneasy feeling that I didn't belong, especially when we were warmly welcomed as the brightest of the bright who would change the direction of education. I suppose we did lay some important groundwork that week. But that night I had a dream. I was at a cocktail party at the Washington Hilton wearing a cozy little black dress and black high heels, as I had done

136

earlier that evening. Someone tapped me on the shoulder and whispered in my ear, "Your rainbows are showing." I woke in a sweat, and when I was approached with interest the next day by one of the *Fortune Magazine* editors, I almost ran the other way in terror of being discovered as a fraud. She apparently saw something in me that I did not.

Years later I would lead the State of Oregon to be the first with a virtual education network, accessible to students across the state on videoconference and then on the internet. I'm proud of these accomplishments and grateful for all the people I met along the way. I look back at that woman with awe.

Memories come and go like flashes of light in the dark. I'm a young girl. I'm in the attic. There were many attics back then, back east, where a sort of musty smell invited exploration into boxes sealed with yellowing tape, boxes folded over with flaps of cardboard, boxes overflowing with old clothes. I am rummaging through a box of old clothes, try them on—rayon dresses of another era. I imagine my mother dancing, twirling, sliding under the arms of someone who has grabbed her and pulled her to the dance floor. Way at the bottom of the box is a yellowing cotton frock covered with eyelets and carefully stitched pleats and seams. This dress had once belonged to my grandmother. It smells of lilac and dust and ages gone past. It smells of expectations and tears, laughter, and the final release of something—perhaps a young girl who accepts her role as a woman.

This young girl, me, has an active imagination and curiosity. Tired of the dresses, I flip open the top of a box of books. Each one cracks with age and unuse as I flip the book open to the middle. It must be one of my father's college books. My eyes catch on a picture of a sprouting seed; perhaps it's a bean. I read how a bean becomes a bean plant in a damp dark place and then grows with sunlight—foliage budding from the bean seed. I learn the word germination. I will keep this knowledge to myself. I'm not supposed to be in here, so I crawl through the rubble to the cupboard-like door, but I am sidetracked by a red leather suitcase.

Snap. Snap. I hold my breath to see what's inside as I lift the lid. The square leather box is lined in gold satin. Matching ribbons lie desolate at the bottom of the empty case. There are pockets held stiff around the edges with elastic stitching. My hand runs through each one. I'm hoping to find something, a clue perhaps. Just as I'm about to give up, I touch something rigid and cold and remove it from its hiding place. It's a gold oval piece of jewelry—a locket with no chain. There is a faint opening around the edges. I work at it with my fingernail, and finally it pops open. Buried inside there are small pictures of stranger's faces. Is that my mother? I look closer. It might be. The other photo is scratched out, scribbled and scraped away—only a faded suit lapel remains at the bottom of the photo. I hear someone coming up the stairs and cram the locket into my pocket, snap the red suitcase shut, and wriggle out the door. Someone, I don't remember who, will want to know what I've been up to. I probably hid that treasure so deep I don't remember ever seeing it again, but I do remember my young mother's face in the photo, beaming and happy.

As time wore on, I dragged things retrieved from the attic downstairs or to my bedroom. I couldn't stay away. In the summertime it would be so hot in there you could hardly breath; in the dead of winter my fingers would freeze as I grabbed hold of the old Smith-Corona typewriter, a book called *Evangeline,* my father's navy uniform—bell bottom pants, a button-up flap in the front, a matching wool shirt, a collar trimmed in white stripes. Best of all, there was a white Navy hat whose brim would turn up or turn down in all sorts of directions. I liked to wear that hat with Dad's old glasses from college. I imagine one day I was caught wearing the clothes and typing, one key at a time, my fingers black from the ribbon, the glasses falling down my face. I imagine I was scolded. One day I came home from school and faced my mother rocking in an old family chair. Her frown turned to tears when I entered the room. When my father came home from work, she told him my teacher called to tell her I was a deeply disturbed child. I have since figured out that was a figment of someone's imagination.

A creek ran behind our house. When we moved there, my father warned me never to put so much as my big toe in that water. I'm pretty sure I never did. But that didn't keep me away from the fields of grass at the end of our street and the sloping forest on the far side of the creek. You had to cross a trestle to get to the woods. I loved and feared the precarious crossing.

It's a summer afternoon, and without warning, I am there, I am twelve years old. Frozen where I stand, I swallow, gasp for breath. The boys have already reached the other side and are throwing rocks off the edge of the trestle into the creek. I grip the side girder. I will have to let go if I am to make it across. I'll have to go down the middle, one long even step after the other, like the boys have done and made it look so easy. They are ignoring me now, but if I don't get across soon, they'll tease me. Worse, they will leave me behind—the ninny girl, too scared to cross.

"Go for it," I hiss to myself. I take a step, bring the other foot forward, sway back and forth. "Don't look down. Hold steady." I hear water splash against rocks far below.

I look over at Goose who glances back across the expanse that might as well be a hundred miles. He turns away. I linger in this battle between fear and determination.

Then I run, leap from one railroad tie to the next. About halfway across, I think I hear the mill train. I hold my stride, but a few steps away from the other side, I stop again and wobble uncontrollably. The sound of rushing water pounds inside my head, a fine mist fills my mouth. I wonder which will come first, the fall or the train.

The boys turn, urge me on. Goose holds out his hand, and I make one final leap and grab hold. Shivering like a field mouse after a narrow escape, my feet make contact with gravel. Crisp creek air wraps around me like a blanket of courage. Oh the memories. They come to entertain me when I least expect it.

Years later, I'm at my friend, Nicki's. We're in her office preparing for a tour of Egyptian temples where she will take a few of her students. "Feel that," she said, pulling my hand toward her breast. There is an unmistakable bump, a lump the size of an egg.

"You've got to see a doctor!"

"I will when I get back from Egypt." She says this in a way that does not invite argument. "I need the money. Twenty-some people have signed up for this. I have to go. I'll see my doctor in San Francisco on the way back. I trust him."

I want to cry. I wanted to beg, but I know that Nicki is going to play this out on her own terms. With a lump like that you could be dead next week.

We went on with the business in her office that once was a chicken coop. Jim turned it into a working space decorated with Nicki's mementos from her world tours with the Grateful Dead—to Egypt, to Woodstock, and all points in between.

Once she left for Egypt, I drove up to her place on the top of the southwest hills in Eugene every day to open the mail, answer the phone, pay the bills. I didn't need a job. It was about friendship, about the feeling of being at home in her magnificent garden where the yellow roses and fuchsia-colored dahlias bloomed, where the ancient apple tree held court over the rows and rows of flowers and herbs. I believe she will beat this thing, and she does. We're all on borrowed time.

It's hot. Very hot. I don't know how the crowds of whirlers and twirlers do it. Back stage, there is a cool breeze. MG says, "Come on." Her dog, Kita, a little shepherd dog, is in obeyance on the end of a thin red string. I follow the two of them up a ramp to the back end of the stage. Amazing how much is back here—a refrigerator, an entire living room, carpets. There's a couch off to the side where we take a seat. Johnny Hagen is standing forward near the back of the band and flips me off.

I do the same back. It's a signal of love and friendship between the two of us. Bill Kreutzmann is pounding his drums, and Mickey Hart dances in front of his, in front of a tower of equipment that carries the rhythm to the far end of the field and probably farther than that. I dare to look out over the crowd. Infinitesimal humanity. They sway. Balloons drift above. How do these guys handle this? I've never imagined. The drum solo, magnified by the wall of sound, reverberates even back here. I am in a bubble, a dream, a place of reverence. I feel it up my spine, through the floor. It's the Grateful Dead and I am here, in it. Again, out over the endless throngs I can only now imagine the band's perspective as they play their instruments.

This scene has come to me once or twice. There are others, but I tell no one of this because they would not understand. Johnny was killed in a car crash, Kita is dead. Jerry is dead. The Deadheads persist, as they will long after all of us are gone. That's the beauty of it all.

People have told me to tell more of those stories. Why? I ask. So people will buy your book, they say. Pshaw, as my grandmother would say. They have their own story to tell.

I sometimes remember my first date with Jim. We have driven for an hour to a beach by the Pacific Ocean. He and I edge down a rocky moss-covered cliff, sand gathering between our toes and under our fingernails. We have no idea if it is high tide or low tide, but it doesn't matter. I collect agates and broken sand dollars. Jim finds several that are unbroken. We pile our cache behind an old log, washed ashore.

I feel the burning sensation of too much sun on my face as we wander the shoreline. I let the saltwater soak the bottom of my jeans, I let whatever might have been chomping at my soul dissipate. Later, eating our meager picnic in a patch of sun between rocks and driftwood, the sound of waves splashing against pillars of boulders along the shore provide the background music to our falling in love. There are small moving figures where blue sky meets a sea of almost the same color then imperceptibly melt into the blazing white sand.

As the sun begins to set, I repack the picnic backpack with leftover cheese and empty wine glasses. The distant horizon is colored a crimson red. I feel red hot with this new event, a new love.

I can still hear the gulls, taste the salty mist from the sea. The wind picks up. We retreat to a shelter of driftwood someone has left behind. Holding hands, we gaze at the lights from the beach houses on a distant crag, a sea cliff dotted with homes with warm beds and full kitchens where people are fixed in their lives—safe and, I believe mistakenly, permanent.

Tall grasses wave at us from the edge of the cliff above our shelter. Peering as far out as I can see, I ask, "Is that a helicopter?"

"No, it's a boat. See it bobbing in and out of the waves?"

By now the soft pinks and scarlet wisps of clouds make a final sweep across the horizon, reminding me of a drowning swimmer gasping for a breath of air before going under—an unfounded hope that there might be another chance before the water fills his lungs. Then things happen that we know nothing about. In a matter of minutes, the fiery rim sinks to the other side of the world. The warmth of the sun turns to chill, and he pulls me close.

The sun has disappeared on its way to China. It will be tomorrow there soon. It is dark except for remnants of the day that shimmer on the ocean's surface—a reflection of heaven on earth, and then all the lights from the beach houses fade into darkness. The people are asleep, confident in their world by the sea.

For a brief moment, I feel like a lost sea urchin, but the falling in love fills me with a deep feeling of belonging, even though we are here on a cold beach in the dark, still unaware of the ebbing of life in the future.

I had a reoccurring dream in my 30s. A giant black slobbering bear is on top of me. He has me in his clawed clutches. He will not let me go. I am helpless. He will punish me for all I have done wrong, for everyone I have hurt. I am finally going to pay. I try to scream, but I can't. This is how it will end. I scream myself awake, but it takes time for Bear to disappear. One night, Jim and I are sleeping in our bed next to a sliding glass door that leads to a wooden deck and hot tub. I scream and try to fight off the bear. I roll onto the floor and crawl toward the door. Jim is shouting, "What is it? What is it?" He slides the door open, and I fall out onto the deck. I am safe. I gasp for breath. There is no doubt I have been attacked, and there is no doubt this monster will return for me. Jim holds me in his arms, and for now I am safe.

Bear returns again and again until, at some point, he does not. He may still, but for now I am safe. I am okay. I am a good person, worthy of walking this earth. This understanding is slow in coming. It fades in and fades out.

I am older now. Most of my life is in the past. I am alone. I review the myriad scenes of my life as they enter my consciousness, unbidden. I relive the past like a movie with colorful characters—me in the lead role. Mostly my face is not clear, but I see the girl, the woman, from a perspective of compassion. She is brave, she is funny, she is foolish, she is doubtful at the same time she is certain. I wish she had made different choices, more informed choices, but then the story would be different. My story is wonderful and painful, exhilarating, and sad. I accept it and wake most mornings able to enjoy the simplicity and solitude of the day ahead. A fresh breeze on my face this morning was almost like new love, old love—a feeling of peace that may have always been available, but unknowable. Comfort comes in small waves and discomfort no longer holds much meaning.

There was one more road trip a few years ago.

When Dan asked, I was tempted to go on his proposed adventure. To tell you the truth, I never considered declining when he invited me to ride along on his return camping trip from the East Coast to the Pacific Northwest. He had a big diesel truck and a pop-up camper. He would drive to New York; I would fly, and we'd take the return trip together, sort of a trial run to see how we could get along for more than three days at a time. We'd have fun, see the sights—see the Grand Canyon and some of the national parks I'd never seen before.

I made a mental list of all the reasons why I shouldn't, or couldn't, but I flew to Syracuse anyway. By that time, he had already crossed the prairies and was visiting with his daughter and one of his ex-wives.

I'd spend a few days with my family, and then he and I would have two weeks of uninterrupted togetherness, sleeping like sardines in the tiny bed in his new hard-shell camper. I disregarded a glut of nagging doubts and decided, really, what could go wrong. This would probably be my last road trip across the country—one more chance to see roadside attractions like Wall Drug and the largest buffalo in the world. One more chance to experience the thrill of the onslaught of the Rocky Mountains, the Badlands, endless cornfields, and new exotic places I had missed all those years ago. So I gave in like a sinkhole in a hurricane.

I left my beloved dog, Lily, with my ex-husband and prepared to make the most out of what would surely be my last days with my mother who was losing her memory as constant and as the downward flow of water. I had everything to gain and nothing to lose.

During our final phone conversation, Dan and I agreed to study the atlas together the next time we saw each other; that would be in Upstate New York where we would plot a fun and adventurous cross-country trip. I was All In.

The plane ride, that first night with my brother, and three days with my mother slipped away like a dream. I can barely remember my mother's scowl, the hours spent in the rocking chair watching her live out her days on the sofa drinking Ensure and droning on about her family of origin, the one she hadn't seen in 70 years.

"Mom, do you remember that you have five children and a bunch of grandchildren?"

She'd look at me with a blank stare; glimmers of recognition shaped into frowns. "I don't understand what you mean." She held up the picture of her parents. "These are my parents. Isn't my father handsome?" She pointed to a picture of my own father, her late husband, in his Navy uniform. And that's Pete Cole."

"I know, Mom. He was my dad."

Again, her expression was one of perturbance and confusion. "That's not possible."

My mother always had a wild imagination, turning her unpleasant childhood into cherished memories. We kids would gather 'round and listen to endless tales about the north country, her handsome father who would take her wild bunch of brothers to the woodshed one at a time; he kept his razor strap by the door as a reminder. We heard these stories over and over as if by drilling each scene, each memory, into our young minds would take her back to International Falls. She told them as humorous tales from a past undone but not complete. She was the Will Rogers of mothers, a domestic Dorothy Parker. We could all mouth each of her stories.

Her cast of characters included Uncle Clyde, Aunt Mame; her brother Archie who was in the ski troops during the war; her brother Ray who was known for his temper—"If you saw Ray's neck turn red and it goes up to his jawline, you better get out of the house and run." Her brother, Johnnie, was the closest to her in age, and the nicest. Her older sister Gladys would have her come stay at her place across the border in Canada in the summertime. Edith was a drunk and a ne'er do well. Stories of her parents'—Jack and Ella Coffin MacPherson—lives were endless. She told us stories about the nuns at her school who terrified her, and her friend Elsie who probably was her one bright spot in life back then.

Having grown up in the desolation of the wild country of northern Minnesota, now she lived in the desolation of memories. I listened to the litany about these strangers who had become the mythology of my mother's life and therefore mine. No wonder I have trouble dissecting reality from fantasy. I nodded with all the compassion I could muster. I understood, always, that she had been an unhappy young mother, torn from a family that no longer existed. The MacPherson family had played out their drama long ago in the coldest spot in the US and now over and over in her mind. If she could only return to the crowded table in the little house where older brothers' and sisters' theater unfolded before her young eyes; where her alcoholic father terrorized the lot of them, where young Ethel prayed each night that her sister Edith would behave herself, come home at a decent hour and not sass her father who could be volatile, even when sober.

None of that would come to pass and the year after his death at the height of the Depression, she and her mother and younger brother embarked on a train for Richland, Washington, and a new life. My mother cried the whole way. One time as a grown woman I returned home for a visit and there on the table was a beautifully framed picture of her childhood friend, Elsie instead of pictures of her children. While the people and the life she could never reclaim were ghosts, her five children were but shadows.

We time Dan's arrival in my hometown, my little village on the Finger Lakes, to coincide with a town gathering—fish fry, same local band as 50 years ago, the adored sax player, familiar-looking faces cropped with gray hair. The water is choppy, but a few boats have eased into the slips across from the seafood festival at the old Sherwood Inn across from the lakefront. The band—the one I first danced to in the basement of the Presbyterian Church at the age of 13—is setting up as we circle the block in search of a parking space. My siblings are somewhere in the crowd.

I feel as though the stars, my stars, are in order. That night, he and I spend our first night together in the pop-up camper in my sister's backyard next to the woodpile, meticulously stacked by my brother-in-law. It has been a perfect day. My special friend arrived safely, and we are anticipating, if not planning, our cross-country adventure.

Dan does not seem to be in a rush to leave so we visited with my family and my friends—dinners, beers, laughter, and an evening by the lake at a friend's camp watching the sun set. With a little prodding, I could talk him into moving here to the little village on the Finger Lakes. Fiery reds and pinks melting above rippling waters could induce anyone to stay. I keep to myself the stories about icy snow and wind that will soon advance. Before long, the shores of Skaneateles Lake will be buried and as unapproachable and miserable as the Alaska Tundra. My days in a place I once called home will soon evaporate.

A few days later, we pack the camper and the truck and head 30 miles north to return the car my brother loaned me the day of my arrival. Dan follows me in his truck, and after one wrong turn, we locate the little town next to the last remnants of the Erie Canal.

Following my brother's instructions, I lock the car and wrap the keys in a plastic bag and toss it over the towering, rickety old fence that surrounds his back yard. The keys and the bag float in a sort of slow-motion arc over the seven-foot barricade at the same instant I remember that my bag and my jacket are still in the back seat of his car. Bob will not return from his doctor's appointment until later, if at all.

We try forcing the lock on the gate; wander the perimeters in search of an entrance, finally gazing through a small crack near the gate where the keys lay on the ground next to the picnic table. Fort Knox comes to mind.

I knock on a neighbor's door. A young man with dark hair and a beard opens it wide enough to listen impatiently to my story, my plea for a stool or a small ladder. "I don't have anything like that," he says without sympathy, and closes the door.

I hold Dan's foot steady as he peers over the top of the jagged, pointed, and slivered old wood; it sways back and forth and the ancient fence might as well be a razor-wired prison blockade. No way in.

"Just toss me over," I say. "It's my fault."

"No way . . . your back, you'll hurt your back."

We pace and Dan makes another walk around the borders of the enclosure that keeps neighbor children away from the pool and would-be burglars at bay. We try the front door one more time, and then the garage door. No one is getting in, and we can't leave my bag or my new coat behind.

"I'm going over," he says. And before I can argue the point, he is dangling atop a dagger of a fencepost, about to be impaled unless we can somehow readjust his position. "Hold my foot," he yells from his mortal perch. I'll let him stand on my head if that's what it takes, but he has already wrestled himself free and plunges to the ground on the other side.

A bag of keys come flying over the fence and then Dan—his stomach raw and bleeding. We wipe off the dirt and the memory and head south and then west. Together in the front seat of the big diesel four by four, we will enjoy the time together we'd been anticipating. We are off to see the Grand Canyon and Zion—first stop, the Shenandoah Valley.

We meander through the Finger Lakes in a diagonal search for the best road south. Late morning sun sheds light onto cornfields and cow pastures where I'd grown up and am now eager to share with my Western-born friend. Occasionally, a lake appears near the road and sparkles and shines like a young child on their best behavior. I want to ask him questions I've saved up: Why did he suppose we were together in this truck? Is he interested in digging deeper emotionally, you know, like grown-ups? What is his greatest fear? After one more feeble attempt, he replies, "I don't know the answer to that question." I give up on the potential intimacy of a truck cab.

We eat lunch at a local winery, sample their award-winning Chardonnays, and by late afternoon we are worn down by the day—the fence, the alcohol, and the fact that Dan is already tired out. He's driven more than 3,000 miles, visited with his family and friends, my family and friends, and is now embarking on another visit and another cross-country drive. Perhaps I should leap from the truck like a wise girl scout; instead, I suggest finding a place to camp near the infamous raceway at the south end of Cayuga Lake.

The gatekeeper at Watkins Glen State Park urges us down the road, says there would be camping on the right. We sail past a raft of stores and various outlets for boats and car racing, but no campground. Of course, we are going so fast I don't have more than an instant to make out any of the signs dotting the roadside—a shortcoming of mine I would learn later.

I leaf through the Camping World directory on the seat between us and try to program the GPS. Eventually I learn how to operate this thing through practice, squabbles, furtive lessons while sailing down the road and several near crashes. Sometimes the contraption with the annoying voice leads us to our destination, or at least some reasonable vicinity.

Another winding country road appears to lead nowhere but to yet another farmer's field, but eventually and unexpectedly we loop past a golf course and again I try to read the sign as we fly past. "You just passed it."

". . . a golf course."

"It said State Park on the bottom of the sign." Try turning a large truck and camper around on a country road. Dan will become adept at this maneuver before we return to Oregon.

"Just golf," a friendly and sporty-looking guy in the parking lot informs us, and then he directs us to a campground he claims to be nearby; I stealthily record names and places on the cover of the atlas. The friendly golfer calls his friend who runs the place. I gather this is an introduction of sorts. "I'm sending some folks your way" would be our ticket into the local campground. Some old guy in a polo shirt would be standing at the end of the road, arms spread in grand welcome.

"This can't be right," Dan says. The curvy road narrows, empty of signs or any indication there is a public campground anywhere nearby. I scramble to put something meaningful into the GPS thing. Dan reaches across the seat to check my work. The truck swerves. I grip the door handle, bite my tongue.

We are about to give up, but finally we come across familiar-sounding road markers and the directions I had scribbled down, we find the campground. It is more like a stumbling upon—no one in a polo shirt is here to greet us—no one at all. We wind around unmarked campground roads, stopping in front of a large hunting party of good old boys who direct us to another part of the campground where there will be electricity and bathrooms.

We locate the office and meet the first of a long series of campground hosts who carefully map out, pencil and line-drawn map in hand, where we can set up a pop-up camper for the night. Our criteria include proximity to bath houses, level ground, and a modicum of privacy in which to pee in the dark and have some privacy. We have begun our exploration of the intricacies of local nature from one end of the country to the other, saving our most important discoveries for the Grand Canyon, Bryce Canyon, and Zion National Park. This is merely the runway to a spectacular adventure through the wide land where a brave species of pioneers traversed in covered wagons over 200 years ago. We have a hard-top pop-up camper, a GPS, and a Camping World directory to guide us through the wilds and often confusing side-roads of the USA. The earlier adventurers left dead children in shallow graves along their endless journey in covered wagons and on foot.

That first night on the trail we shake off the perils of the day before and stroll, arm and arm, along the "blue trail," the shorter of the two Dan had selected for his own walk in which I intruded. Halfway around the giant pond, he is being eaten by mosquitoes that don't seem to care for my blood.

We sit down on a bench, placed there just for lovers I imagine, perched on the side of a hill overlooking the large fishpond. A small rowboat rocks gently within sight, fishing poles in the water, a shadow of pink surrounds the little craft, and the sun begins to set. I imagine making love in the carpet of soft green grass, but the remaining day's light hustles toward the horizon on the far side of the lake, and there are those guys in the boat. Just my imagination again.

Upon our return to the campsite by the bathroom, we politely turn down an invitation from a couple of locals, regular campers who stay for three weeks at a time, who set up camp complete with name signs, awnings, tablecloths, and lanterns. I feel a pang of longing for their stability. Before we escape their hospitality, we learn they have been doing this for

39 years and still enjoy the thrill of parking their 21-foot travel trailer in the mosquito-filled woods. "We tried the walk around the lake once, but that's not for me," she says. "Too long a walk for me; I'd rather stay right here."

I crawl into bed while Dan takes a shower and wipe away the tears on my cheeks. I must be tired. Dan returns and snuggles in behind me. He feels cool and his skin smooth. We sleep in each other's arms until sometime in the night he moves to the adjacent small bed.

The next day we meander our way out of New York State, past Corning Glassworks, away from the Finger Lakes, away from my homeland, and head into the central valleys of Pennsylvania. All day long we follow the Susquehanna River through familiar-sounding names of Civil War towns and battle sites. Like New York, tourists are targeted by wineries, Amish museums, and other roadside enticements. People like us look for remnants of times gone by. We agree to travel secondary roads where we might find cafes and roadside stands, the kind where moose heads and hubcaps and license plates cover the walls; where old-timers rock in Shaker-built chairs on front porches—happy to see strangers appear in search of a taste of local fare.

We pull in at the Welcome to Pennsylvania rest stop and fill our arms with brochures jam-packed with places to learn about the Civil War, apparently now the stuff of tourism and nostalgia.

The longest river in the eastern United States, the Susquehanna River, flows from New York through Pennsylvania, Maryland, and on to the Atlantic Ocean. The road shadows its banks, seen and unseen. By the time the North Branch and the West Branch make confluence, about a third of the way through the river valley, our stomachs are rumbling. As navigator, it is also my job to locate the best places to eat—the most interesting with the best and most affordable food served by someone whose family may have settled this valley. We want local; we want genuine. It won't be until later in the trip I discover I like McDonald's coffee mocha frappes. Don't ask me what a frappe is. It's sort of a milkshake without the milk, available at every interstate rest stop from New York to Portland.

"Those two rivers are flowing in different directions," Dan says as we sail past a series of restaurants. I'm supposed to pick one, but he's going too fast. The Susquehanna is definitely flowing in a southerly direction now, and so were we, and frankly, I don't care at this point. A fifties-style diner appears about 20 feet from the side of the road ahead. I don't want to take a chance that this will be the last watering hole before Maryland, so we agree on the direction of the river's current and our lunch stop. We eat prepackaged hamburgers and club sandwiches and soft ice cream. We both try to avert our eyes when a man, whose crotch area fills one entire chair, laps up a giant hotdog smothered in something I assume is edible and must include cheese and beans. I'll never be sure.

I pay for lunch, per our agreement, and head outside to the restrooms with a key bestowed by the cook, waitress, and cashier—a bouncy young girl in her twenties. I make an effort to not think about the germs in these situations, and my attention is diverted soon enough by the cautionary sign on the bathroom door about customers only and shoot-on-sight warnings. On the way back inside, I stumble upon a box filled with badminton rackets, tennis balls, and birdies. Two nets flutter in the breeze on the wide lawn, just past the outside seating area—one for badminton, one for volleyball. I haven't played anything that requires a net since childhood. Dan needs some cheering up, I think. He is tired; I can feel his mounting frustration. The guy has been on the road for over two weeks.

I hold out a racket as he emerges from the country-style fifties-era diner. "Badminton anyone?"

He doesn't turn me down but is in no hurry to relinquish the potential handicap of wind and blaring sun; I lose the toss and we batter the plastic bird over the net, one serve at a time, running, or limping, to retrieve the plastic relic, vying for one return lob. With the sun in my eyes, I can't tell if he's chucked one back, but I'm not going to argue. Despite our full stomachs and aching backs, we have a little fun and I relinquish the title. We pull back onto Highway 15. We will make Winchester by dinnertime.

Three-quarters of our trek through the rolling and endless green hills of Pennsylvania, we abandon Route 15 and the zigzag course of the Susquehanna River for the interstate heading for the state line and Hagerstown, Maryland. From there, it will be a short hop into Virginia. Except for the lunch and the badminton, my day has been one long bumpy ride struggling to focus on the road map, to set the GPS for the next destination, to convince Dan that he could drive, and I could be trusted to lead us in the right direction. Bumpity-bump. My aging eyes try to focus on the tiny keypad and the lines on the map. What kind of struggles had Robert E. Lee faced when he attempted to traverse Confederate troops across the Susquehanna River into Maryland during the Gettysburg Campaign in 1863? Would a GPS have helped him avoid the opposing militia? I doubt it. Might these men have missed their operation squabbling over the best way to program their destination into a devise that would deliver their route from 12,000 miles above the atmosphere? Their battle was on the ground, as is our mounting mêlée, but those soldiers in gray and blue most likely kept their eyes on the trail and the river.

We plan to be in Front Royal, a historic town nearby Winchester, Virginia, by nightfall come Hell, or flood, or Union soldiers. We have been invited to stay for two days with a high school acquaintance of mine and his wife. My friend mentioned in his last-minute invitation that his wife was from Thailand and a very good cook who will prepare authentic Thai food for us that night. The following day we'll explore the Shenandoah Valley, take a drive through Shenandoah National Park.

Our destination is at the confluence of the north and south forks of the Shenandoah River. By nightfall, and thanks to the help of GPS—whom I have taken to calling Gertie—our bellies are soon filled with the best Thai food either of us have ever tasted, Dan having once lived in that country.

The following morning, well rested after a night in a real bed wider than two and a half feet, our host fulfills his promise, and we drive along Skyline Drive where once in a while I can see the river meandering through a leafy valley where the color green takes on a singular rainbow affect—an ecology of emerald, jade, forest, lime, olive, and avocado. Dan snoozed in the backseat of the Toyota hybrid, probably grateful for the rest and the distance from his navigator. Had I felt a rupture between us begin to form the way it does when the ground rumbles deep inside right before a flash flood?

Within two days' time, I have the opportunity to examine the life of someone I haven't seen since high school—like peering into a stranger's lit picture window at night—and then we head west, away from the eastern seaboard and toward our destinations in the southwestern USA. I've never seen the Grand Canyon, never experienced places like Zion or Bryce Canyon. We'll make haste across the plains but try to take enough time to enjoy each other's company, share the tiny bed, and to explore the picturesque countryside through which we drive. There is still a measure of time to enjoy the winding off-interstate roads through West Virginia and Kentucky where quaint farms pepper the landscape.

By midday, after what feels like a full day of winding and bumping along a two-lane highway, zigzagging through West Virginia in the big pick-up truck, camper in tow, we are ready to escape the byways and make haste on an interstate heading south toward Huntington, Kentucky, by nightfall. Hot and tired and eager to find a place to pop up our little hotel room on wheels, it is about 4:30 when we pull off the highway to fuel-up, a handful of miles from the state border. A long line of cars at the BP, Dan's gas station of choice, forebodes a waste of time. People are gassing up for Friday night. We opt for a quiet-looking station down the road in Barboursville. My idea. Soon we'll have another full tank of diesel fuel and make headway into Kentucky.

"K-Y!" I shout. There's something about the impending end of a day on the road that evokes a surge of energy and cheerfulness for the road weary. Dan eases the big rig parallel with the pump and jumps out—more of a skid onto the pavement. I feel his weariness—his energy drained; I know he is dog-tired, battered, done-in by endless miles of winding roads up and around and through a monotonous green paradise, and by my endless chatter. Another time, he may have feigned interest in my soliloquy about the evils of the BP Corporation. Had he rolled his eyes, or was it just the blaring afternoon sun?

I stay in the cab, study the map and the camping guide. Engine cut, the AC gives way to furnace-like heat. I consider asking him to roll down the windows, but this pit stop will only take a few minutes. If we hop back onto I-64, we might make it to some pristine spot in the Daniel Boone National Forest by nightfall—maybe catch sight of a bear or a bear of a man clad in a coonskin cap. I begin pasting sticky notes next to promising campsites in our three-inch thick directory of roadside watering holes.

I open the door, but it's hotter outside than inside the cab. My back hurts and my stomach is growling. Dan explodes there by the pump. "Oh shit!" He hollers. Not the kind of oh shit I just stubbed my toe; not the kind of oh shit I left my wallet in the car, but a rendition of Oh Shit no one wants to hear in a gas station on the outskirts of Huntington, West Virginia, late in the day on a boiling hot Friday afternoon. I hold my breath; wait.

Five minutes pass and no sight of Dan. I see only his back when he dashes into the Quik Mart. I slide down out of the truck until my toes touch the asphalt, and then lean forward and hug the side of the seat. Maybe he's gone inside to pay up, so I send a few text messages back home. Jouncing down the highway is not conducive to texting, writing, map reading, or much of anything for that matter. God, my back hurts.

Where is he? I send photographs from my cell phone of
our stay in Virginia to everyone on my contact list who might
be interested. Hasn't he been gone longer than it would take
to pay for gas, use the John, or buy some coffee? I strain to
see what he's up to through the gas station window. I watch as
people, then more people, come out the door. Maybe he's using
the bathroom. Maybe he's stopped up. Maybe he lost his wallet.
I lean against the seat, stretch my back and my aching legs.
Sweat trickles between my shoulder blades. Then he appears as
fast as he disappeared. "Stay with the truck!"

"Sure," I say and turn to touch him, to find out something,
but he is gone again. After a while I climb back inside and
close the door; unable to open the windows, I have to get
outside again in order to breathe. It might not be a bad idea
to stretch my legs, so I saunter around the truck and the
camper—about 50 times before I see him heading toward me.
By the look on his face, I'm thinking this must be a serious
case of travelers' constipation.

He rattles it off. Spits it out, perhaps in hopes of ridding
himself of the reality of what he has done. "I put gas instead
of diesel in the tank! The handle is green. In Oregon, the
handle for diesel is green. I put gas in the tank." As the pitch
of his voice increases, my understanding of the severity of
what has happened begins to sink in. I don't dare ask questions.
I might ask: What does this mean? Are we getting out of this
godforsaken gas station any time soon? But I keep my mouth
shut.

He vanishes again. My sauntering turns to pacing. What
is he doing in there? Has he just said that if we had only
gone to the other gas station, as he had wanted, this wouldn't
have happened? No. Who would say something like that in a

situation like this? As I consider this, I realize that perhaps I would. Perhaps the first reaction, for some of us, to a crisis of this magnitude, is to find someone else to blame. I will never, ever, do that again. I have done it before.

Dan is apparently using the phone book and the phone inside to find a car rental place open at 6:00 p.m. on a Friday in western West Virginia. I retreat to a neighboring liquor store and watch through the window as Hurricane Towing glides into our pit stop gone bad. A gnarly guy with muttonchops is at the wheel. He guides his giant rig in for the rescue with practiced precision. I run from the liquor store without the beer I have been sent to buy, and stand by the truck, wait until Chuck tells me to get inside. I climb up and over and into the tiny back seat filled with greasy tools, used fast food wrappers, and an assortment of garbage, gears, riggings, and the kind of paraphernalia a tow trucker might need or have discarded or saved.

From my perch in the backseat, I catch bits of Chuck's diatribe, slurred in a local drawl, or his personal version of the English language which is difficult for me to decipher. He is telling Dan a story about why they don't let campers stay the night at the local Walmart no mo' because of trouble with prostitution. "Good thing they didn't know about the camper at the dispatch desk,' cause they wudda charged ya double."

"I'll call and thank her . . ." Dan is grateful for a penny saved; I watch the sweat dripping down the back of his neck.

"Notta good idea."

Chuck, with one final master maneuver, backs the camper into one of two open spots behind the dealership's service center, and then lowers the truck into the last one available spot. It starts to rain as I pull my bags from the back of the truck and wait for Dan to settle the bill. We walk across the parking lot toward the Hampton Inn.

I let my emotions wash away with the sudden rain. Dan's tension is enough for us both. I stand in silence while he pays for the overpriced room. No, there are no senior discounts and they have met their quota of veteran's discounts for the month. I wonder what exactly that might be. All I want is at least one alcoholic beverage as soon as possible, but we discover before long that the chain restaurant next door serves only soda and iced tea—we're in a dry county now.

It's nearly 3:00 o'clock on Monday afternoon when we pull away from the Jeep dealership in Huntington, West Virginia, and a weekend in a hotel room we will both probably try to forget. I have no idea what we did there—if we touched each other or were able to find words of comfort or compassion. I take it personally as we resume our trek.

We beat our way through Kentucky bluegrass country, sticking to the interstate, trying to make sense out of what just happened. At one point he yells at me, "I'm not made out of money!"

I search the map for cheap campgrounds on the other side of the state. We'll make time. Things will be OK. We're on I-64, and shades of green blur with billboards covered with horses and bottles of bourbon as we dash past. There are long rows of white horse fences. That's all I remember now.

It's nearly sundown when I suggest we stop. He wants to press on, to drive until there is no driving left. "Let's not push it or make any important decisions late in the day," I urge. "There's a campground at the next exit; I'll call for directions."

We struggle with exits, directions, and wind up in a field of RVs next to a cornfield in the middle of the Kentucky heartland. From here on out, we will begin in earnest to find cheap campgrounds and level parking spots close to the bathrooms with flush toilets and showers. That is all we can hope for now. I try to be helpful, but all I have to offer is my presence, a meal at some point during the day—leftovers and beer as the setting sun points to our destination. I can't shake the feeling that I've done something wrong, that this is my fault.

We befriend a young couple living by the cornfield in a handmade Tiny House on wheels. I am brought to tears when the little girl—about the age of Iris when her father and I built her special loft in our tiny house bus—ushers me up the ladder in her tiny house where she lives with her parents and siblings next to the cornfield. She presents her loft, pointing to everything she has in the world that makes her happy.

I remember older couples coming inside our bus-house back in the day, ruminating on how fortunate we seemed, how they wished they could live that simply and be that happy and in love. I remember the curtains from Iris's old loft I stumbled upon only a few weeks ago in my trunk of old treasures. When I return to the pop-up across the way, I shed more tears and then return to the business of trying to have a good time. I feel an emptiness where just days ago there was hope and anticipation. Is my imagination playing tricks? They say that men are from a different planet for which women have not broken the code.

That night we plot the fastest route back to Oregon, set our alarm for five a.m. I lie in my bed and stare through the window at the night sky over the freshly mowed field of corn, listen to crickets and comfort myself with the soft glow of starlight. The night air is colder than it has been. A chill descends over the camper. So much for the Grand Canyon.

We fly like geese in a flurry of late migration through Illinois, Nebraska, Iowa, Utah, Wyoming, and then Oregon. I hardly can recall the exact order. I do remember watching in silence as we kept pace with the Platte River, with urgency through Sandhill Country, transitory throughout the day, our stops short-lived. In one last attempt for a side-road adventure, we take Route 30 out of Grand Island, Nebraska. We argue about the map, about exits, about my ability to read the map, about nothing important and everything important. The blazing sun endures.

In Wyoming we find a refuge in an unexpected old BLM campground while making a slapdash side trip toward a pay-park 20-some miles farther up the road. We are like fugitives hurling past towering bluffs and glacier-carved hillsides when the open gate and picnic tables along the riverside catch my attention.

The place is empty; rows of abandoned campsites sit fallow, nestled there beneath a rust-red bluff alongside a rippling bantam river. This was the day of our first real fight, the first fight, and maybe the last. We have both been thinking this. But here was a good sign. Here is our refuge and our first stroke of luck since the gas station incident.

I am still suffering from the effects of 72 hours nonstop with my mother, Dan from endless hours of road-time, of meeting new people, visiting family and old friends, and now trying to have a good time with me. We had a beer with lunch in Laramie—one of those high-octane craft beers my nervous system can't endure depending on unknown variables like hormones and sleep deprivation or an extended visit with

Mother. After lunch, on our way back to the truck, he grabs my shirt, pulling me from the side of the road where he apparently senses danger. To me, it feels like one of those slaps on the back from my father that would knock me off kilter when I didn't see it coming. I react—react badly. What happens next happens so fast, I don't remember the words—something from me about the Golden Rule, something from him about mistreatment, possibly deserved by men in my past. There are tears, shouts, and the kinds of recriminations that can't be easily retrieved. We riddle each other with emotional shrapnel.

"Treat people the way you want to be treated!" I shout. He roars words meant to hurt in return. I swipe at the tears pouring out from the rims of my sunglasses. It remains one of those moments we all have that we wish we could erase, like the moment right before a head-on collision, the moment before a doctor tells you it's terminal, before the child falls from the tree.

"This will never work! I don't trust you!" He bellows on, and I cry, and then we try to soften the blows by telling each other with a new shared language of hurt and fear about the events of our lives that made us both so raw. Perhaps it is only I that say these things. He suggests I return to my counselor. He tears at my shirt to demonstrate what a real thrashing would feel like.

Despite this act of violence, I need to turn this around, to return to something lost and forget what this new thing has exposed.

But now—here in this little paradise, our stroke of luck, our second chance—we strip bare and wade into the water, holding steady against the current and the invisible lacerations from the day.

By the time the moon rises above the shadow of the blazing sun against the rim of the bluff overlooking the cool river where we washed our bareness, we lay in each other's arms. Gazing up at the bluff, I imagine a scene from an old cowboy movie; tops of heads, rifles or arrows emerging like a herd of wolverines come to spy down on the interlopers.

We leave before sunup, returning to the interstate river, passing Sinclair, Wyoming, and its small collection of oil refineries. A moon so bright it could have been the sun rising in the west hangs over the horizon toward which we are headed.

"Let's find you some coffee," I say as I try to steady my camera to capture the light of the moon.

"We'll get some fuel and maybe find you a coffee-mocha frappé?" he says.

The photographs I took that day at a roadside attraction off the Lincoln Highway in Utah turn out upside down and I've never been able to right them. They remain capsized in my hard drive, like the Titanic. We abandon plans for sightseeing farther north in Wyoming. "I just want to be home," he says. That does not include me.

Our final night on the road, our last campsite, is at Mike's Recreational RV Camping. It's too close to the interstate on one side and bounded by railroad tracks on the other. Our check-in sheet says that there is hardly ever a train on those tracks and not to worry about a disturbance; to use a penny buried in the sand in an ashtray next to the toilets to get inside—this to keep out the bikers and other riffraff. Mike asked us if we needed sleeping pills, propane, or whisky.

"We're good on all counts," Dan says, "but stop on by if you want to partake . . ." We shower before bed, and, breaking the check-out rule on Mike's list—Mike the former cop who hates bikers and probably other minority types too—we leave before daylight.

We never saw the Grand Canyon, Bryce Canyon, or Zion National Monument, or much of anything else other than the inside of that Dodge truck. And like a blazing sunset, our friendship faded into the green hazy mist of the horizon through which we stormed like a dozen locomotives.

After he dropped me off, I pieced together the tragedy of what became the end of what had become, for me, an imperative, and for him, a burden he could no longer endure.

It was, once again, time to go.

Epilogue

What defines a life? Memory has a way of playing tricks. We may feel as though we've failed, and then one day we are thankful for the lessons and wisdom we've gained along the way. We seek to untangle the chaos. The self evolves while it conquers its inner conflicts. We try. We fail. We try again. I am still trying, but have finally learned to listen to my heart, to be more observant. For most of my life, I felt unlovable. Now I am loved—by my dog and by myself. Camille—*nee* Nancy—is okay. She can take care of herself, and she must learn to set boundaries.

We all fear. We operate with fear until we learn better—not only through our own experiences, but what we observe in others, especially the ones closest to us. My parents feared shame—the kind they might bring upon themselves, or the kind their children might bring upon them. My grandparents feared death—the unexpected kind that takes children in the night, or in the middle of the day when they are crossing the street. On that day long ago when I crumbled to my knees in the middle of the road having pushed Jim's car over a cliff, I had scratched at the wounds and fears of the sum of growing up Nancy. What was it I was so afraid of, a beating? The loss of love? That I may have hurt someone? Was I in trouble? Was I going to get it? What?!

We regret. Does all the garbage in your wake mean you led a bad life? That you made bad decisions and hurt the people you loved most? I believe the living of a full life teaches us compassion and sympathy, especially for ourselves. The corners fill with the meaning to which we've ascribed our own mythology.

We feel the ache of nostalgia. The loss of what and who we have loved. Have we loved well and been loved in return? These are judgments that change over time, judgments and memories of the places and people left behind.

We resent. We resent what has been inflicted upon us—the betrayals, the hurts, the bad luck. I had the lead role, right? Did I listen to my heart, or did I simply assume that things would turn out true to my expectations?

We long. Longing is a pain in the sternum that demands to be fed. Some feed it booze, or drugs, or sex. Others understand it for what it is and seek a higher truth. Now I long to spend my time in peace, at peace.

Best of all, we love. And the nature of that love changes over time. When we're little girls or boys, we don't dream of romantic love and white knights. We dream of stallions, big, gleaming roan-colored ones with glistening haunches. We imagine ourselves galloping across high deserts gulping sagebrush wind. In the heat of the afternoon, we tie our stead to a fallen tree by a river's edge—warm sun on our face. We are in the moment in a way that we'll struggle to learn how to do again when we're adults.

And if we've lived a good life, we have loved deeply. We've learned to forget—learned compassion, to keep our distance from those who we understand will hurt us.

Before Jim died, he said that he'd come to understand, with certain death looming, that life is about learning to love.

A life is a story—the actual events, the story we tell ourselves, the story we tell others, and the story that one day resolves as the story of our life. Elements of it are based on fact—the rest is the fiction of our own mythology that changes over time. To make sense of the chaos, we look for the balance between who we are, who we want to be, and what has been lost in the fury of time. Memory is a creative process, not a storage process. Who is to judge? How do we make sense of the senseless?

The author of many wonderful books based on a life of loss and love, Amy Tan, says, "I write about secrets, lies, and contradictions, because within them are many kinds of truth."

We are forever leaving or losing something, someone, or someplace. Every morning, yesterday is left in our past, in our wake, in our hearts. Some will be remembered with clarity—a smell, a song, a pain in the center of the chest. I once heard someone say that all love ends in tears. One way or another, I suppose it does.

As of this writing I am 73 years as this person. As I go through my days, a sound, an aroma, a tap on the shoulder can evoke five minutes or five seconds of my past; the sound of an ancient tree creaking in the wind; the clang of a cowbell, of many cowbells; a flag flapping in the wind, in the breeze of a summer afternoon; someone crying, me crying. "Memories are like moonbeams—you do with them what you want," said Bobby Darin in a movie of his life of the same name.

Home is on the inside—where your passion lies. In time, one rediscovers the small comforts of a room—a basket filled with soft yarns, a collection of beads; a little dog, a fire crackling in the fireplace—a certain stillness.

Life itself is a destination we never reach until we die. It's about what happens along the way, and what we learn from those experiences. We are all different, and we are all the same.

As children we are left in the dark for our own good, left to piece together fragments of tragedies—like the time my best friend died when I was about five; I heard them all weeping downstairs, but I never found out what had happened. I wondered where he was but was afraid to ask. I did ask about 30 years later and my mother was shocked at my memory. No matter how old or how young, we take it all in and process it the best way we know how.

Sometimes there's an empty echo in my chest—a yearning; a need to fly and sing above the trees. It shouts, "Feed me!" I believe we all have a void we try to fill—we want to feel loved for exactly who we are. I believe that when we are children, we see ourselves and the world through our parents' eyes. Once we enter the world, we see ourselves through our friends or our teachers' eyes—try to be who they want us to be, who we've convinced ourselves and them that we are. If we're lucky, we come to know and accept who we really are. One way or another, most of us survive our pratfalls, like diving into a wild river and barely missing an underwater boulder, over and over. We are all wild creatures in our own unique way.

I've lived my whole life making live or die snap decisions—jumping out of a moving car—hasty bets on the workings of a complex and mysterious world. Sometimes I tucked when I should have rolled. Most of the time, I believed I failed to fit in, failed to domesticate.

We live complicated lives in a convoluted universe. The human brain, say scientists, is a network of a hundred billion neurons shooting information from one center to another in utter chaos. We are slick machines without a highly trained operator. We rely, in many circumstances, on our instincts. The key is to listen to those instincts.

Some call it free will, some call it fate. I have at last learned to pay better attention to my alchemy. But I, like you, are capable of narrow escapes; take a quick dip into the Akashic records and the tomes of mythology. Has it all been figured out, or are we are each making it up as we go? We do have the gift of insight and intuition—the ability to allow the rational mind to get out of the way. The secret to the tuck and roll is to do it with confidence.

One day you wake up and everything has changed. Sometimes it feels like the weather behind is as bad as the weather in front. Life knocks us over. Life is a stage act, like the Midnight Show. All the players are characters for you to remember the way you will. He was a cowboy; I was an actress.

About the Author

Photo by Rachel Hadiashar

Camille is the author of two books for classroom teachers and a narrative non-fiction account of her great aunt's life—a renowned educator.

She has published short stories, articles, book reviews, and a monthly column. Once upon a time she wrote a monthly serialized satirical soap opera about life in Oregon, *As the Rain Falls*.

The Midnight Show is Camille's debut memoir. She lives in Portland, Oregon, with her dog, Lillian Albright—Lily.

MORE BOOKS FROM GLADEYE PRESS

The Time Tourists
The Yesterday Girl
Sharleen Nelson
Follow the adventures and mis-steps of time-traveling PI Imogen Oliver as she recovers lost items and unearths long-buried stories and secrets from the past in this exciting series!

Tripping the Field: An Existential Crisis of Un-godly Proportions
Ian Jaydid
Empiricist scientist, Professor Michael Huxley tumbles, stumbles, strides, and crawls through the jungles of South America, the mountains of Tibet, and the backwoods of Colorado in search of enlight-enment and the hope of saving the world from a religious cult that has discovered a dark shortcut to the power of quantum realities.

10 Takes: Pacific Northwest Writers Perspectives on Writing
Jennifer Roland
From novelists to poets to playwrights, Jennifer Roland interviews a variety of authors who have one thing in common—they have all chosen to make the Pacific Northwest their home.

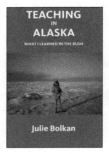

Teaching in Alaska
What I Learned in the Bush
Julie Bolkan
Among the first outsiders to live and work with the Yup'ik in their small villages, this book tells Julie's story of how she survived culture clashes, isolation, weather, and struggles with honey buckets—a candid and often funny account of one *gussock* woman's 12 years in the Alaskan bush.

 **GladEye Press**

All GladEye titles are available for purchase at www.gladeyepress.com, in book stores, and from Amazon.com

Dying to Win
Patricia Brown

Even a bucolic beach town has its skeletons. When the newly wed husband of the area's richest heiress mysteriously disappears, Eleanor and her friends find themselves entangled in dark secrets involving bullies, racists, murder, anonymous love letters, and more!

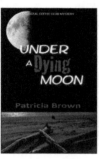

Under A Dying Moon
Patricia Brown

When a young girl washes up on the beach, there is no doubt murder is once again the topic in town. Two more brutal murders bring the town to the edge of panic. Are the newly arrived young swingers involved or the cute retired couple? And what is the deal with the gnomes scattered around town?

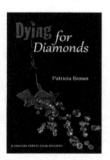

Dying for Diamonds
Patricia Brown

When a mean-spirited mystery writer visiting her sleepy coastal town is murdered, Eleanor Penrose, her retired detective friend Angus, the coffee club ladies, and Feathers, the irascible African grey parrot, work to solve the puzzles without becoming the murderer's next victims.

A Recipe for Dying
Patricia Brown

The old people are dying in the small coastal town of Waterton, but no one seems to notice—after all, that's what old folk do, isn't it? Eleanor and her delightful assortment of friends, most whom are getting up in age, set out to discover what is going on. Is it a series of mercy killings, or murder, and is their investigation putting them in danger?

COMING SOON from

 GladEye
Press

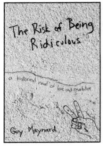

The Risk of Being Ridiculous: A Historical Novel of Love and Revolution
Guy Maynard
Join 19-year-old Ben Tucker for a passionate, lyrical six-week ride through confrontation and confusion, courts and cops, parties and politics, school and the streets, Weathermen and women's liberation, acid and activism, revolution and reaction.

Look for Maynard's second book coming soon.

Faith, Hope, and Dying
Patricia Brown
The fifth book in the Coastal Coffee Club Mysteries series follows Eleanor as she investigates infidelity, murder, and long-buried secrets in the sleepy seaside town of Sand Beach.

Available May 22, 2023.

Visit www.gladeyepress.com for fantastic deals on all GladEye Press titles.

Follow us on Facebook: https://www.facebook.com/GladEyePress/

GladEye titles can be ordered from your local book store and Amazon.com.

CPSIA information can be obtained
at www.ICGtesting.com
Printed in the USA
BVHW050918260623
666386BV00002B/4